A House Divided

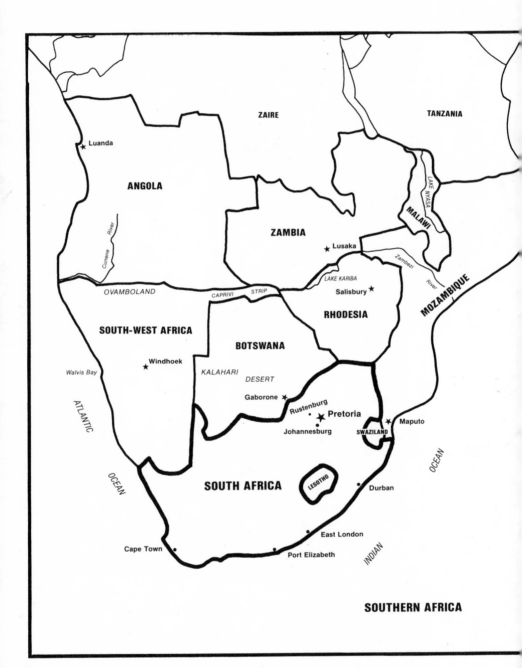

SOUTHERN AFRICA

A House Divided:

South Africa's Uncertain Future

John de St. Jorre

CARNEGIE ENDOWMENT FOR INTERNATIONAL PEACE
New York   Washington, D.C.

Two of these essays, each in a somewhat different form, have appeared elsewhere. "White Citadel" appeared in the October, 1976, issue of *Foreign Affairs* under the title "Inside the Laager: White Power in South Africa," and "Retreat into the *Laager*" appeared in the Fall, 1977, issue of *Foreign Policy* under the title "South Africa: Up Against the World."

I.S.B.N. 0-87003-009-4

Library of Congress Catalog Card Number: 77-87410

Printed in the United States of America.

Contents

Preface

In the opening years of the 1970s, U.S. policy toward Africa was a policy of not-so-benign neglect. Our official view until recently was that American interests were minimal and in any case adequately protected by a state of inertia brought about by the success of African nationalism north of the Zambezi and its failure south of it. A succession of important events in southern Africa in the mid-1970s and a new administration in Washington in 1977 have changed all that.

The unfolding African drama began with the coup in Lisbon in April, 1974. The subsequent collapse of the Portuguese empire in Africa—500 years of colonialism wiped out in as many days—dramatically reduced the boundary lines of the supposedly solid white south. The Angolan civil war which followed in 1975 introduced an unexpected and ominous degree of internationalization: South Africa and the West embarrassingly on the side that lost, and Cuba and the Soviet Union unashamedly on the side that won. The momentum generated by the demise of the Portuguese produced a new sense of urgency about the need to solve the outstanding colonial problems of Rhodesia (Zimbabwe) and South-West Africa (Namibia). The African nationalists' military struggle intensified, helped by increased Soviet military aid. Independent black Africa, especially the key "frontline" states, became more militant. The West, in response to fears of "another Angola" and the dawning realization that all the Cassandra-like predictions of a race war in southern Africa might materialize, stepped up diplomatic efforts to promote negotiations between the contesting parties.

South Africa, once comfortably cushioned from regional pressures by the white buffer zone and protected from undue international aggravation by a blandly acquiescent American administration, suddenly found itself deprived of both allies. As the supplier and supporter of beleaguered Rhodesia and the colonial administrator of South-West Africa, the Republic is inescapably involved in shaping the fates of those two countries. But, for the first time since the Sharpeville shootings in 1960 and the period of political and economic instability that followed, South Africa's own future began to look uncertain.

Two additional factors have heightened the sense of uncertainty and growing isolation. The black students' revolt which started with the Soweto demonstratons in June, 1976, revealed the strength and determination of the black consciousness movement. This stirring of the urban masses is unparalleled in black Africa and will undoubtedly have important consequences in the future. Second, the Carter adminstration's commitment to meaningful political change aiming at eventual majority rule in South Africa, and a new willingness to put pressure on Pretoria, even while the South African government's cooperation is being enlisted to settle the Rhodesian and South-West African problems, is an unusual departure for American policy, both in concept and in execution. Africa, along with the Middle East, is now visibly high on Washington's foreign policy agenda.

Underlying the administration's thinking on South Africa is a basic reappraisal which has resulted in a reversal of President Nixon's "tilt" towards Pretoria, a process which was documented in another Carnegie Endowment book, The "Tar Baby" Option by Anthony Lake. Far from being viewed as the West's bulwark against communism—the traditional perception shared by Pretoria and many Western political and military strategists—South Africa today is seen as a major liability in the attempt to check the growth of Soviet influence in southern Africa. Also, the expanding influence of the black constituency in the United States, combined with the racial polarization that is taking place in South Africa, has sensitized Washington's policy-makers still further to the dangers of being or even appearing to be on the wrong side of the black and white battle lines which are being drawn in the Republic. In the supposedly hard-headed business of assessing the country's national interest, the volume of U.S. trade and investment (Nigeria's oil is a major component) is also growing faster with black Africa than it is with the white south.

The purpose of the Carnegie Endowment's International Fact-Finding Center is to study pre-crisis situations which carry significant threats to international peace. The instability of southern Africa in general and the dilemmas that face the South African government in particular merit research and analysis. This study by John de St. Jorre, a former Africa correspondent of the London Observer, concentrates on the problems, hopes and pitfalls that face governors of the Republic. Based upon the author's lengthy field trips to South Africa, the five essays present a profile of the white and black power structures, an assessment of Pretoria's political and military strategy in Africa, a detailed account of how the South African government is striving to make the country more self-sufficient in armaments and in fuel, and an examination of the options open to Pretoria and the West in the critical period that lies ahead. St. Jorre concludes that there may still be a focus for Western policy-makers in striving to strengthen the middle ground in South African politics before antagonisms finally harden. But he argues it is unhelpful for the West to prescribe precise solutions to South Africa's unique problems. Pressure, not prescription, is what is needed, and the time-scale is short.

However, given the West's limited leverage, the chances of producing radical changes in Pretoria's policies are remote. St. Jorre does not expect South Africa's vital interests such as its supply of oil from Iran, or its capacity to buy arms, or the role of gold in the world's monetary system, to be affected by Western action. He is not optimistic about a change of heart by the South African government over its apartheid policies. The independence of Rhodesia and South-West Africa under black governments will intensify pressure on Pretoria and exacerbate the divisions between white and black in the Republic. If the center fails to hold, civil war is inevitable and the most likely outcome in South Africa is neither apartheid nor majority rule but partition. A *House Divided* reveals that serious partition blueprints are already being drawn up by leading Afrikaners who feel that life in a truncated South Africa will be more acceptable than the prospect of black rule.

As always, the Carnegie Endowment's publication of this report implies a belief only in the importance of the subject. The views expressed are those of the author. We are pleased to present another timely and stimulating piece of original research.

Thomas L. Hughes
President
Carnegie Endowment for
International Peace

"Our house is not built on sand."
— John Vorster, Prime Minister of South Africa
New Year's Eve, 1977

"If a house be divided against itself, that house cannot stand."
— Mark 3:25

Introduction

Writing about southern Africa in the late seventies is like trying to catch water in a sieve. Opening the newspaper in the morning becomes a hazard: another fact, assumption or hypothesis has been devalued. Since the collapse of the Portuguese empire in Africa, the pace of change in the southern portion of the continent has accelerated rapidly while the last pockets of colonial rule—Spanish Sahara and Djibouti—have been removed in the north. The white buffer zone which protected South Africa for so long and which appeared to have halted the sweep of African nationalism on the banks of the Zambezi is disintegrating. Angola and Mozambique have gone, Rhodesia and South-West Africa will follow. By the end of the decade, there will, in all probability, be only one white-ruled country left in Africa, the Republic of South Africa.

I started this study with the whole southern region in mind, but as the dramas of Angola, Kissinger's shuttle-diplomacy, Smith's majority rule gyrations, the abortive Geneva conference and the twists and turns of Anglo-American initiatives on Rhodesia and South-West Africa flicked past like so many brilliant but ephemeral frames on a fast-moving film, I decided that it would be safer, if perhaps less immediately topical, to concentrate solely on South Africa. There was a certain satisfaction in this because the Republic differs in many respects from the other white-ruled countries of Africa and because its complex racial make-up and absorbing history would make it a fascinating study wherever it was located geographically.

But it is, of course, geography that endows the country with a special interest. At the tip of Africa it witnessed the flow and, inevitably, the clash of two great migrations: the Dutch (and later the British) from the south and the Africans from the north. South Africa is perfectly placed to act as sentinel over one of the world's major sea routes, and beneath its soil lies great treasure: gold, uranium, diamonds, chrome, iron and coal. Its ports, factories, farms and cities give it an economic power and a sophisticated appearance unparalleled on the continent of Africa. And yet by American 1 standards, South Africa is not a large country, its surface area only marginally exceeds the states of Texas, New Mexico and Oklahoma combined.

In the view of its white rulers, South Africa's strategic location and mineral wealth are not the only claims it has on the West. Historically, too, the whites trace a connection and a responsibility. Cape Town was founded in the same year as New York and by the same people, the Dutch. The Afrikaners, the white tribe that developed from those early settlers and now forms two-thirds of the 4.3 million white population, still see themselves as the guardians of an outpost of Western Christianity and civilization. They are often genuinely puzzled and hurt when Europeans and Americans refuse to share that vision. The parallels between the early Cape settlers and the Calvinist-inspired Puritans who came to New England and between the Boers who went on the Great Trek and the pioneers who opened up the West are, to them, glaringly obvious. The Afrikaners also assert that they have achieved a true sense of nationhood through the trials and tribulations of imperial oppression and internal division and that they have had to fight every step of the way during three long centuries of turbulent history to survive.

What makes the situation especially poignant, as black nationalism in South Africa moves into a more dynamic and threatening stage, is that the Afrikaners' victory is relatively recent. It was only in 1948, with the National party's triumph at the polls, that the Afrikaner nation became politically united and moved into power. It still took another eleven years to cut the final link with the old enemy, the British, when Dr. Hendrik Verwoerd, the South African prime minister, narrowly won a hotly-contested referendum and declared the country a republic outside the British Commonwealth of Nations. And the still sensitive nature of Afrikaner unity was demonstrated in 1969 when a small but determined group of right-wingers broke away under Dr. Albert Hertzog, a cabinet minister and son of one of Afrikanerdom's greatest heroes, to form a rival party which has continued to challenge the ruling Nationalists on the central issue of how to deal with the black population. As an Afrikaner academic has pointed out, "The Afrikaners are the only group in our South African society who have experienced both the pain of subjection and the joy of liberation."

The real dilemma for the Afrikaner now is how to reconcile his own freedom and identity with the undoubted right of the black and brown peoples of South Africa to a similar degree of self-determination. Ever since the Afrikaners first clashed with the Africans in the eighteenth century, the story of South Africa has been a struggle over land and power. With the defeat of the Zulus and Xhosas by first the Afrikaners and then the British in the 19th century, the protagonist—but not the prize—changed with the white men fighting each other and the Afrikaners being defeated in the Anglo-Boer War in 1901. The country was given independence in 1910 with the struggle unresolved. Within two years of that date the Africans formed their first political movement, the African National Congress, while Afrikanerdom remained divided, part of it supporting a coalition with the English who ruled the country, the rest clinging to a purer vision of ethnic exclusivity in opposition. While the Afrikaners and the English contin-ued their historic joust in the political arena in the 1920s and 30s, the Africans were kept in a cocoon which effectively, though not in an ideological way, deprived them of any hope of a fair economic and political share in the common society.

The Second World War exacerbated divisions among the Afrikaners but brought the country into the conflict on the side of the Allies and later enabled its leader, General Jan Smuts, to play the role of world statesman as a founding member of the United Nations. However, the majority of Afrikaners distrusted his domestic policies, and his English-Afrikaner coalition was defeated by the vehicle of Afrikaner nationalism, the National party, in 1948. The new government instituted a new order: apartheid to keep the blacks in their place and the progressive entrenchment of Afrikaner power to fend off English encroachments. Successive elections have consolidated the Afrikaners' political position and enabled them to institutionalize the separation of the races.

After three decades in power, Afrikanerdom still has only one solution for black aspirations: the Bantustan policy. Its greatest flaw, apart from its being imposed by one group of people on another without adequate and representative consultation in the name of "separate but equal freedom," is that it entails a grossly inequitable division of land based on the Land Act which has not been substantially altered since its enactment in 1936. Thus the Bantustan policy leaves 87 percent of the country and its resources in control of 16.5 percent of its population. Many thinking Afrikaners recognize the contradiction between their own belief in identity, freedom and nationalism and their steadfast denial of these same concepts when expressed by their black countrymen. They also realize that the era of *baaskap* ("crude white domination") is past, being neither practically nor morally defensible, and that the African (not to mention the Coloured or the Indian) shares a basic humanity and aspires to the economic and political goals that the whites have already achieved. The great problem for South Africa, and it is essentially a problem for the Afrikaners since they hold the heights of power in everything that matters, is the resolution of that contradiction.

The essays in this book cover a fairly wide terrain and are essentially reportage. What I have tried to do is to give a view of what is happening in the Republic and how the people who live there think and react.

A large number of South Africans, black, brown and white, have given me their time in interviews and discussions while I was collecting material for this book. I owe a special debt to the South African missions in Washington and New York which were most helpful. During two prolonged visits to the Republic in 1976, no hindrance was put in my way. To all these

4 people, officials, politicans, academics, lawyers, businessmen, students, theologians and journalists, I would like to extend my grateful thanks.

The largest debt of all, however, is to the Carnegie Endowment for International Peace which, through its innovative International Fact-Finding program, made this study possible. The basic aim of the International Fact-Finding Center is to fill the void between journalism—by its very nature short-lived—and academic writing, inevitably slow and out-of-date by the time it appears. This alone is an exemplary concept. But it becomes even more valuable when the people administering it combine skill and understanding. I would like to thank Tom Hughes, the Endowment's president, and Bill Maynes, the former secretary of the Endowment, for their encouragement and guidance; Diane Bendahmane for the arduous production job of turning the fragmented pieces into a polished whole; Susan Fisher for diligent typing and creative editing; Vivian Hewitt, Jane Lowenthal and the rest of the Endowment's library staff for finding everything I wanted and much that I didn't know I wanted until it appeared and filled a gap I thought would never be filled; Rich Ferguson and Peggy Hanson for making the administrative side of life so much nicer than it usually is; and Margaret Ameer Cataldo for everything.

John de St.Jorre
New York
September, 1977

CHAPTER I

White Citadel

"The storm has not yet struck. We are only experiencing the whirlwinds that go before it," Prime Minister John Vorster said in his New Year's speech in 1977. An earthquake metaphor might have been more apt, for there had been tremors beneath the white redoubt for a year or more before the South African leader hoisted his storm signal. The edifice swayed perceptibly under the shocks of an unsuccessful military adventure in Angola, prolonged black upheavals at home, a faltering economy, escalating guerrilla wars in Rhodesia and South-West Africa, and the steady alienation of Western friends. Hairline cracks appeared in the superstructure, and they may have deeper origins; but the foundations of white authority were unimpaired.

White power in the Republic of South Africa is Afrikaner power. Settled in the country since the seventeenth century, the predominantly Dutch forebears of today's dominant white group were pushed into the interior by the English during the Napoleonic Wars and defeated by the latter in the Anglo-Boer War. Since then, however, with their tight-knit ethnic strength and numerical predominance, the Afrikaners have gradually taken over political control and gathered increasing economic strength in the Republic. Their political arm, the National party, has held the reins of government firmly since 1948.

It was on the anvil of British imperialism that the Afrikaners first forged their nationalist armor. Afrikaners retain a revolutionary image of themselves. Unlike the English, French, or Portuguese in Africa, they turned their backs on their European origins. In search of land and solitude, they swept north in successive migratory waves and clashed with black tribes pushing south. They were not innovators but a practical people who had a talent for modification. They fashioned a religion out of Calvinism and a language out of seventeenth-century Dutch. The church and Afrikaans remain as pivotal to Afrikaner nationalism today as Judaism and Hebrew do to Zionism, although their racial ideologies are entirely different. They regard themselves in all seriousness as Africa's first freedom-fighters—against

5

British imperialism—and although they lost the war, they finally won the peace.

In all *volk* history there are distortions and myths, but they do not necessarily weaken the faith of the believer; on the contrary, they often reinforce it. However, the power of what has been called the Afrikaners' "civil religion"[1] has waned since its zenith in the 1930s and 1940s. And there is today no conclusive agreement on the identity of Afrikanerdom or the role it should play in modern Africa. There is, in fact, constant debate and much internal divisiveness. Yet the symbols and the institutions of a durable nationalism are there. The purely ethnic content of Afrikanerdom is certainly being eroded by the need to pull in the English in order to present a unified white front to the black threat. And although the inspirational view of Afrikaners as the chosen people of an omniscient God has receded into obscurantist backwaters, there is no lack of consensus, of moral righteousness, or of will when it is a matter of who should guide the destiny of the twenty-six million people of South Africa.

While the Afrikaners are, like the Rhodesians, undoubtedly a minority group defending their privileged position against an impoverished and unrepresented majority, at the same time, and quite unlike the Rhodesians, they have, through a slow and painful process lasting 300 years, evolved as a distinct ethnic group. The English of Rhodesia and South Africa and the Germans in South-West Africa still have a European home of sorts. The Afrikaners have none, other than the empty land they occupied and the settled land they bought or conquered. This fact adds a measure of determination, ruthlessness, and perhaps, in extremis, flexibility to the Afrikaner psyche. Afrikanerdom is based on the reverse principle of European and American (or African) pluralism; that is, in order to survive, it has to exert total and exploitative power over rival nationalisms, if only to guide them to a compatible destiny. Despite their self-conscious act of amputation from Europe, Afrikaners still look with some anguish toward the West for a portion of their physical and psychological needs—weapons, investment, protection, and approval. However, Vorster's government is doing its best to reduce this dependency.

The English-speaking community, roughly 40 percent of the white population, has only a marginal impact on South African politics. The English, through the press and Parliament, are highly vocal and they wield influence through their domination of industry and commerce. But they have no political power, nor have they any prospect of achieving it in the foreseeable future. There are several reasons for this. First, as a minority they cannot hope to oust the Afrikaners under the present electoral system, provided the latter remain united and as long as nonwhites are excluded from Parliament. The effective electoral power of the English is less than it appears because relatively few of the large number of English-speaking

immigrants have taken out South African citizenship. In 1974, Piet Koorn-
hof, minister of sport and immigration, said that only 42,000 immigrants out of a total of 400,000 since 1961 had become citizens. Also, if emigration begins to pick up as life becomes more difficult, it will be the English rather than the Afrikaners who will tend to go.

Second, a process of realignment is going on among the English opposition parties. The fortunes of the United party, for so long the "loyal" opposition, have declined steadily, some of its supporters moving leftward to the Progressive-Reform party and others, in the opposite direction, to the ruling National party. The increased gravity of the country's position has spurred a process of polarization. The old adage that the English talk Progressive, vote United party, and privately thank God for the Nationalists has lost some of its validity. Closet Nationalists and Progressives are tiptoeing cautiously out into the open as the days of wine and roses come to an end. (The same process occurred in Rhodesia during the last decade, leaving the center ground sprinkled with the corpses of moderate politicians and their good intentions.) In the wake of the black upheavals in 1976, the South African opposition parties attempted to build a united front but failed. Six of the United party's right-wing members of Parliament were subsequently expelled, and, after abysmal results in provincial and municipal elections in 1977, the United party dissolved itself. A new grouping, pledged to giving non-whites a greater political role in a federal constitution, has emerged calling itself the New Republican party. It will attempt to rally moderate English and Afrikaner votes against the National party.

A third factor is the nature of the English electorate, which tends to be torpid, conservative, and apolitical. The large influx of disillusioned white immigrants from other parts of Africa in recent years has strengthened the reactionary ingredient in the community. The idea that industrialists and businessmen, being practical and farseeing people, represent a major fulcrum for political change seems to be as illusory in South Africa as it has been in Rhodesia, although some individuals, such as gold and diamond magnate Harry Oppenheimer, never give up urging meaningful reform. A confidential survey of 3,000 leading businessmen in South Africa in 1975 showed that the group remains conservative, the greatest support for the status quo coming from those in the top echelon of management.[2] Finally, Vorster's personality has done much to fragment traditional English political loyalties. His strength and pragmatism appeal to the English voter, and opinion polls give him a steady 80 percent backing of the white electorate.

The historical enmity between Afrikaners and English in South Africa has diminished considerably in the last three decades. The consolidation of political power, the urbanization of the Afrikaner, and unprecedented material affluence have blunted the prickly spines of Afrikaner nationalism. After the founding of the Republic in 1961, former Prime Minister Hendrik Verwoerd began to encourage the concept of a white South African nationalism in which the English were to be drawn closer but still held at arm's length from the sacred institutions—cultural, religious, and political—of Afrikanerdom. Vorster has continued the policy with greater energy but not without strong criticism from the ethnic purists in the Afrikaner right wing. The group that has been most willing to reach out toward the English is the expanding body of young Afrikaner businessmen and technocrats. They find it relatively easy to identify with their white compatriots, whose affluence they now share and whose more relaxed lifestyle they admire and emulate.

But underneath the Afrikaner skin there still lies a wariness of the English—for their capacity to undermine the unity of the *volk*, for the assimilative power of their culture, and, in times of crisis, for their suspect loyalty to the country. There are also the abrasive barbs of English opposition which never cease to hurt, although they do no substantive damage. These come, with varying intensity, from three different directions: the English-language press; the English universities (especially Witwatersrand and Cape Town) and the National Union of South African Students; and from the small but active Progressive-Reform party in Parliament.

An indication of Afrikaner mistrust is the government's refusal to capitalize on the undoubted support it has among the English electorate in order to accelerate even the limited domestic reforms it believes to be necessary. On the stump, the National party pays an exaggerated amount of attention to the threat from the Afrikaner Right, when it is usually clear that whatever is lost in that direction will be more than compensated by support from the English Left. The crucial determinant, of course, is the ethnic origin of those votes. In this context, Vorster is no different from any other leader of the *volk*; a single Afrikaner vote is still worth half a dozen English votes any day of the week.

Afrikaner power in South Africa rests upon a number of traditional institutions all closely intermeshed at the top. It is hard to detect a breath, let alone a wind, of change in the taut rigging of the three Dutch Reformed churches, the Afrikaans Cultural Federation, the women's organizations (Afrikaner womanhood, the victim of Zulu massacres and British concentration camps, remains an important symbol of ethnic probity and purity), the state-controlled South African Broadcasting Corporation, the white trade unions, and the powerful fraternal organization, the Broederbond ("Band of Brothers"). There is, of course, debate and sometimes anguished dissent, particularly among the younger generation in the churches and universities. Except for the Afrikaans Calvinist Movement, whose chairman has spoken out strongly against government policy, at the *leadership* level of the organizations themselves, there is no swelling movement for reform; and although they no longer play such a central role as they did when the Afrikaners were consolidating their political power, these institutions perform a dual function of filter and sounding board for Nationalist policy as it descends from the cabinet and party hierarchy.

The Broederbond, in particular, is important here. Founded in 1918 as a way of resisting British influence, it remains the watchdog of Afrikaner life. With a total membership of about 10,000, it is organized on a regional basis consisting of 400 cells or divisions and a central coordinating council which meets regularly in secret. Members are elected and must be Afrikaner Protestants, belonging to one of three Dutch Reformed churches, who send their children to Afrikaans schools and universities. While members may admit their own affiliation, they may not reveal the identity of others. There are Masonic overtones: special handshakes, secret words, and signs for recognition. There is a chairman, an executive committee, a junior wing, and a central exchequer (the Christiaan de Wet Fund, which has more than $1 million in its coffers to finance special activities). Prominent Afrikaners in all walks of life, including cabinet ministers and other leading politicians, belong to the Broederbond.

Some of the secrecy that formerly cloaked the organization was dissipated by a series of revelatory articles by Hennie Serfontein in the Johannesburg *Sunday Times* in 1973 and 1974. However, its role of surveillance over Afrikaner morality and coordination of Afrikaner interests has not changed. The Broederbond also reflects the policy and personality struggles that periodically trouble Afrikanerdom. In 1969, when Albert Hertzog, a cabinet minister, led his followers into the political wilderness to form the right-wing Herstigte Nasionale party, Vorster himself conducted a purge and ejected them from the Broederbond. Another conflict occurred in 1974, when the conservative chairman of the Broederbond, Dr. Andries Treurnicht, was replaced by Professor Gerrit Viljoen, a moderate, again through the active intervention of the prime minister.

The power of the Broederbond is now widely thought to be less than it was; its high point was reached in the 1920s and 30s when Afrikaner nationalist fervor was at its peak. But it would be wrong to relegate it, as some observers have, to the category of an "Afrikaner employment agency," a kind of British public school old-boy network or American Eastern Establishment, with the inference of declining or peripheral power. No major policy issue escapes its scrutiny; some originate from within its ranks. In 1971, the Broederbond worked out a secret policy for sports in South Africa, anticipating with remarkable accuracy the pressures that would be brought to bear against the government from abroad. Two other controversial issues, the future of the Coloureds and racial discrimination ("petty apartheid"), are constantly being chewed over by the Brothers, usually with inconclusive results.

The only area that receives less than microscopic attention is foreign diplomacy, which Vorster has made his own preserve. But even here, the Broederbond has sensitive antennae—especially in Rhodesia, where there are 30,000 Afrikaners, many of them farmers in the embattled eastern frontier zone, and in South-West Africa, which has a similar number of the *volk* scattered throughout that huge, sparsely populated territory. There is a network of cells in each place. In Rhodesia there is a special section called the Genoodskap van Rhodesiese Afrikaners, which contains five branches and includes several important members of the ruling Rhodesian Front and at least one cabinet member. The organization provides a convenient channel for all supporters of right-wing orthodoxy, including some sympathizers of the Herstigte Nasionale party who escaped the purges in 1969 and 70.

The institution with the greatest power, the National party, is also in the doldrums, immoblized by the ideological dispute between the *"verligtes"* and the *"verkramptes."* It is important to place their disagreements strictly in the context of Afrikanerdom's self-interest. *Verligte* ("enlightened") does not mean unadorned liberalism any more than *verkrampte* ("narrow") signifies straightforward reaction, for the first implies openness within carefully defined limits and the second contains a streak of right-wing radicalism. The bone of contention between the two is not the shape of South Africa's future but the manner in which it is achieved and the pace at which changes should be made. Many analysts, including some Afrikaners themselves, shrug off the *verligte-verkrampte* struggle as a charade. However, the ideological fissure it has produced in Afrikanerdom is showing signs of widening.

The *verligte* vanguard is to be found in the Afrikaans press, the universities, the think tanks, and the quasi-government research institutes. There is a great flurry of activity: seminars, writing, talking, planning. The *verligte* intellectuals see themselves as loyal Afrikaner nationalists with a pragmatic bent, as ethnic fair-dealers, and as humanists who reject racial discrimination and domination. Their historical view is that the era of crude racial despotism in the 1950s under Nationalist leaders Daniel Malan and J. G. Strijdom gave way to the ideological apartheid of Verwoerd in the 1960s, then softened into Vorsters's separate development in the 1970s which will eventually in turn lead to a generally accepted ethnic pluralism in the 1980s. Power-sharing and any form of political integration is as abhorred by them as it is by the *verkramptes.* Majority rule is out. But separate development, they stress, must be an innovative, dramatic policy imbued with a pioneering spirit and conducted with self-sacrifice.

They talk of a breathing space while Rhodesia and South-West Africa attract the limelight. During that time, the government must seize the initiative and build up the Bantustans ("tribal homelands") which will eventually become independent black states; move decisively to eradicate racial discrimination; give the urban blacks a better economic and social deal; find a solution for the Coloureds, who have no homeland; and launch a genuine dialogue with nonwhite groups. Long-term plans are less precise. They envisage a patchwork of black and white states linked by federal or confederal structures in which the urban blacks—the biggest problem—will have a significant measure of self-government and perhaps even become small city-states linked at one level with their homeland governments and at

another with the white cities from which they can never be wholly detached.

Verligtheid, as one Afrikaner analyst, F. van Zyl Slabbert, has pointed out, is not a movement. Nor does it have a recognizable leader. It is a collection of individuals with similar ideas on the future of South Africa, although the degree of their enlightenment often varies from issue to issue, e.g., a Cape Nationalist may be *verlig* on the Coloureds but not at all *verlig* on the problems of the urban blacks. Also the thrust of *verligtheid* within Afrikanerdom is not against the political primacy of the Afrikaner but against those who look backward to cultural purity and ethnic chauvinism. It has little real muscle and has to rely on the intellectual caliber of its adherents and the influence they can exert in high places. Its strongest platform is the Afrikaans press, in which the campaign for reform is being led by the respected editor of *Die Transvaaler*, Willem de Klerk, the man who coined the terms *verligte* and *verkrampte* in the mid-1960s. Since the Soweto riots, other Afrikaner newspapers have swung behind Klerk in a veritable clamor for change.

The *verkrampte* view is that there has been enough change for the time being and that change in itself can be the thin end of the wedge: a social or economic concession to the blacks today will lead to a political one tomorrow. Separate development is fine but it must proceed cautiously; racial discrimination can be eased but only in areas where the process will not cause "friction"; and the cultural exclusivity of Afrikanerdom must be preserved at all costs. Regardless of what happens outside South Africa, the government must maintain firm control of the nature and the pace of change. The forces of *verkramptheid* are large and powerful. They number several seasoned generals: Cornelius ("Connie") Mulder, minister of information and the Transvaal party leader; P. W. Botha, minister of defense; and M. C. Botha, minister of Bantu administration and development. There is a solid cadre of officers and non-commissioned officers in the ranks of the civil service and police, and a broad phalanx of foot soldiers among the blue-collar workers in the cities and the farmers on the dusty *platteland*. And Andries Treurnicht, Viljoen's predecessor as chairman of the Broederbond is the high priest.

A former Dutch Reformed pastor appointed deputy minister in 1976, Treurnicht published a book called *Credo of an Afrikaner* setting out the orthodox conservative view of Afrikaner nationalism with its stress on Christian values and ethnic exclusivity. Of separate development he wrote: "I know of no other policy which is so moral, so scripturally justifiable as [this policy] for the diversity of nations." His inclusion in the government in 1976 was something of a shock, since he replaced a popular *verligte* in the important Ministry of Bantu Administration. Conventional wisdom has it that Vorster was boxing him in, although it is agreed that this tactic can sometimes boomerang. *Die Burger*, the Cape Nationalist paper, refused to review Treurnicht's book—not so much for what he said as for his assumed motive in saying it, that is, playing up to the right-wing gallery. Few Afrikaners would deny, however, that Treurnicht articulates a deep and legitimate stream of feeling within Afrikanerdom and that he can muster formidable stopping power against any policies that run counter to the *verkramptes'* concept of their own self-interest.

The National party retains its monolithic appearance, buttressed by its crushing overall majority of seventy-one seats in Parliament. But the *verligte-verkrampte* divide is becoming more anguished. Jan van Eck, editor of the Progressive-Reform party's Afrikaans journal, *Deurbraak* ("Breakthrough"), and a close observer of Afrikanerdom, believes that "for the first time since the Hertzog breakaway [from the Nationalists] in 1969, we are witnessing a serious rift in the National Party. Vorster is in the middle. He knows that if he moves too far to the left he will antagonise the right. As a result the Party leadership is standing still."[3] The Afrikaans press has clashed openly with *verkrampte* members of the government, notably Treurnicht and his supporters, and has been disappointed to see Vorster placing himself at the right-wingers' side. The black upheavals in 1976 have spurred *verligtheid* into a more aggressive posture to the point of confrontation with the government, causing confusion and anxiety in the upper reaches of Afrikaner society but not much more than a ripple below.

Criticism of the government's immobility has also come from other directions in the Afrikaner establishment which are neither strictly *verligte* nor *verkrampte*. The historian F. A. van Jaarsveld, who in 1970 wrote a school textbook widely regarded as expressing orthodox National party doctrine, declared that his countrymen had allowed the political initiative to slip out of their hands in 1976. "The Afrikaner," he said, "stands before an approaching and inevitable war, and he stands alone."[4] Professor Tjaart van der Walt of the Afrikaans Calvinistiese Beweging ("Afrikaans Calvinist Movement") in Potchefstroom has warned that unless fundamental social change designed to improve the lot of the Africans is implemented, more and more Afrikaners, as Christians, will find themselves unable to support the government. This organization, which contains members of all the Dutch Reformed churches but is dominated by the smallest and most liberal of the three, has urged that the Mixed Marriages and Immorality Acts be scrapped. Its opposition to the government's race policies is based on religious grounds, a significant development for a community in which the church is still a central institution in its daily life. Criticism has also come from the direction of one of apartheid's proudest institutions, the black University of the North at Turfloop. Its rector, Professor Johan Boshoff, a respected Afrikaner academic, called for radical reform in the relationships between white and black and challenged the core of the system by saying in a 1976 interview in *Die Vaderland*, "Equal but separate is the most humiliating form of discrimination." Another influential Afrikaner, Piet Cillie, editor of *Die Burger*, appeared to be challenging the core of separate development itself. He argued when interviewed that blacks should be given "full citizenship" rights in the urban areas, though under questioning he qualified this by calling it "co-equal citizenship" for "responsible" people, that is, a limited franchise, at least in the initial stages. Even the Broederbond's Viljoen has spoken out. "Segregation for segregation's sake doesn't make sense," he has said. "Apartheid is not an ideology nor a dogma. It is a method, a road along which we are moving and [is] subject to fundamental reassessment."[5]

The National party is not unchallenged in Afrikanerdom. The men who run it and strive to maintain its defenses have to look constantly to its flanks. On the Left are a handful of radical Afrikaners like Dr. Beyers Naudé, director of the Christian Institute, and André Brink, the writer, who believe that in a head-on collision between Afrikaner and African nationalisms, the former will eventually succumb. Naudé, an outspoken critic of the government, declares that black rule is inevitable and the sooner the whites accommodate themselves to the idea the better it will be for all the peoples of South Africa. Naudé, a former minister of the Dutch Reformed church and member of the Broederbond, is regarded as a traitor by most Afrikaners.

The Right, although still minuscule in numerical terms is more threatening than the Left because its appeal strikes straight at the breast of the *verkramptes* and provokes a deep neurosis in the leadership, which is aware, as all Afrikaners are, of the historic divisions in the *volk* and of their fatal effects. For example, Albert Hertzog (the son of a former prime minister), Jaap Marais, and others in the Herstigte Nasionale party are regarded by many Afrikaners as a lunatic fringe, yet they undoubtedly exert an influence out of all proportion to their numbers. The party made no impact in the 1970 election, was almost annihilated four years later, and still has no seat in Parliament. However, it has been increasing its vote in by-elections since 1974, though never presenting a serious electoral challenge to the National party, and remains vocal and active. Its message is twofold—historical and emotional. It points out that separate development has loosened up society and given black critics, like the Bantustan leaders, platforms they never had before; it is time to tighten the circle of ox-wagons, and the Herstigte Nasionale party with its crusading brand of ethnic nationalism, is the party to do it. Hertzog says, with logic, that if the government's policy is truly based on ethnicity, then the Coloureds and Indians should be given their own homelands, too. If not, then the blacks should be entitled to a *single* united Bantustan.*

"What the Herstigte Nasionale party says in public a third of the Nationalists think in private," an Afrikaner political correspondent told me in South Africa, and most analysts there agreed that it represented a fair assessment. Fear of the Right is a constant in white politics in southern Africa—and with good reason. In Rhodesia, the movement of power to the

---

* He used to talk of a "homeland" for the English but now says he no longer fears that the Africaner's cultural identity will be swamped by his fellow whites.

Right has become an iron law. Hertzog and Herstigte Nasionale party leaders point to precedents in Afrikaner history for successful assaults on the citadel from the same direction and say they are prepared to wait: the forces of conservatism they represent will triumph in the end.

The Herstigte Nasionale party has considerable nuisance value, especially over issues such as the future of the whites in Rhodesia and South-West Africa. The line that it was criminal of the government to send South African boys to their deaths fighting for Africans in distant Angola while they were not allowed to defend their white kith and kin in neighboring Rhodesia is heady stuff on the stump. It is a theme that will be repeated as the situation deteriorates in Rhodesia and will find an echo in the hearts of many *verkrampte* Nationalists. Two chords that have a resonance of menace for National party leaders are Hertzog's claim to Verwoerdian purity—Hertzog was a minister in Verwoerd's and Vorster's governments—and his appeal to all supporters of the cruder *baaskap* version of white supremacy. Hertzog asserted in an interview that as the racial divide becomes dramatically defined, many more Afrikaner and even English voters will turn to the Herstigte Nasionale party.

At the helm in South Africa is the solid figure of John Vorster. The levers of Afrikaner power are firmly in his hands and behind him on the bridge stand a few trusted lieutenants. Understanding the process of decision-making in South Africa has been compared to Kremlinology. It is indeed a mysterious business in which the government often seems to move one step forward and then two back, in which ideology plays leapfrog with practical politics, and in which the self-interest of Afrikanerdom is the deciding but not always the most visible factor. The prime minister, sixty-one years old, has spent a life steeped in politics. He is one of the generation of Afrikaner politicians that vividly remembers the days when the *volk* was divided, when the English were still the enemy. Black power is now the antagonist and Vorster knows a lot about that, since he made his name as Verwoerd's law-and-order man at the Ministry of Justice in the early 1960s. But he can never forget that he was the leader when Afrikanerdom split in 1969 over the alleged liberalism of his racial policies and that his hold on the right wing of his people will only be secure as long as he can satisfy their conservative instincts and aspirations.

Vorster himself entered Nationalist politics from the Right and he knows only too well that the ammunition for an attack from the Right is piling up. Concessions linked to the black riots (albeit minimal, such as scrapping Afrikaans as a medium of instruction in African schools and shelving the rent increases in Soweto after renewed demonstrations by the students), too fast a pace in removing "petty apartheid" practices, "softness" in dealing with black critics like Chief Gatsha Buthelezi, the Coloureds' stubborn refusal to accept the government's halfway house for them, the way Vorster handles the delicate problems of Rhodesia and South-West Africa—these are some of the nerve centers which Vorster's critics constantly probe to his own and the government's discomfort.

Where does Vorster himself stand in Afrikanerdom? He seems to have two basic positions. In foreign affairs he is with the *verligtes*, a supreme realist ready to take risks and meet the changing world face to face. His détente policy in Africa, his rationale for the Angolan intervention (fighting for his African allies in order to achieve an *African* solution, an Angolan government of national unity), the stern advice to Ian Smith to get on with majority rule, flexibility on South-West Africa under Western pressure—all these developments attest to Vorster's adaptability and all have been opposed at varying levels of intensity by the right-wingers.

In domestic affairs, however, his stance is enigmatic and hard to define. He is not *verkrampte* but neither is he *verligte*. On internal change he moves slowly, elliptically, with great caution. He endorsed the famous statement by his ambassador at the United Nations in 1974—South Africa does not condone discrimination on the basis of color—but he would also agree with Connie Mulder, who said on the removal of discrimination, "You can't have a blueprint, you've got to play it by ear." South African domestic policy sometimes appears to evolve by a process of osmosis, rather in the manner in which Tory party leaders used to be chosen in Britain: something finally emerges. Apartheid ideologues will be satisfied with the framing of a law, and separate development pragmatists will be content with its less than rigorous implementation. Playing both ends off against the middle is a minor South African art form; thus the inevitable can be satisfactorily disguised, as in the erosion of job reservation—the system which bars blacks from entering a range of skilled and semi-skilled occupations—and the upward mobility of black labor.

The key to Vorster is that he is an authoritarian who believes first and foremost in control and then in applying the power at his hand in subtle shifts this way and that according to the balance of pressures. He represents a return to a more traditional kind of Afrikaner leadership after the sternly ideological Verwoerd. If one had to tie a label on him in this context, I would favor the tag recently used to describe the present chairman of the Broederbond: a pragmatic conservative. Vorster strives for consensus, but it is a cautious business; and if there is strong disagreement or risk of division, he will shelve the issue or employ delaying tactics. This preserves a balance in the cabinet between men who represent the various political and ideological differences within Afrikanerdom: Piet Koornhof, the *verligte* minister of sport and immigration; Mulder, the hard-headed Transvaal party chief; P. W. Botha, the defense "hawk" and National party leader in the Cape; and M. C. Botha, of Bantu affairs, Verwoerd's loyal disciple. But the style also appeals to the prime minister's own character and to those close to him, such as Van den Bergh of the Bureau for State Security, Viljoen, and Hilgard Muller, the former foreign minister.

Many *verligtes* privately say that Vorster lacks the qualities of leadership and creativity needed for the crisis that is coming, that as a man who is now in his sixties he is too locked in to his past. The trauma of the split in Afrikanerdom that occurred in 1969, when Albert Hertzog and the extreme Right broke away, lies heavily upon him and he is in no mood to alter the stream of Afrikaner history at this late stage. The men who criticize him thus—Afrikaner editors, academics, businessmen, a growing number of politicians—are beginning to look beyond his craggy countenance to his eventual successor, who will probably be a man of their own generation, someone in his forties. The problem here is that the candidates whom the *verligtes* favor tend, as they themselves do, to lack political weight.

The heir apparent remains Mulder. His image is *verkrampte*, but there is a small coterie of *verligtes* close to him who say that he is a flexible and pragmatic man and will surprise his critics if and when he comes to power.

The other man who has been steadily building up support in the last year or so sends shudders down good *verligte* spines. He is Andries Treurnicht, still outside the cabinet in a deputy ministerial post but already the standard-bearer of ideological *verkramptheid*. There are other leading politicians who cannot be excluded from the succession stakes—P. W. Botha, for example—and the quickening tempo of crisis may yet produce surprises. The *verligtes* have their own friends in high places, notably Piet Koornhof, and Chris Heunis, minister of economic affairs; but neither wields the political clout necessary to make a serious bid for the leadership. If Vorster were to step down tomorrow (an unlikely prospect), Mulder would move into his chair without difficulty. In early 1977, there was a confidential poll of the National party parliamentary caucus, the body which chooses a new leader when the post becomes vacant. Two-thirds voted for Connie Mulder, the rest for P.W. Botha; Treurnicht was not considered because, as a deputy minister, he was ineligible. But the longer Vorster stays, the greater the threat Treurnicht will pose. Some of his supporters are already billing him as the true successor to Verwoerd, a man of pure principle and inflexible will who might even eventually heal the wound in Afrikanerdom by bringing back the Hertzogites.

Treurnicht made some significant progress during 1976. His appointment as a deputy minister early in the year* was followed in September by an easy victory in the Transvaal party elections to a seat on the Federal Council, the politburo of the National party. In any future cabinet reshuffle, he is a promising candidate for a ministerial post, possibly balancing *verligte* Roelof ("Pik") Botha's elevation to the Foreign Ministry. Treurnicht is a Transvaaler—the key province in South African politics—and looks considerably younger than his fifty-six years. In addition to his clerical background, he has been a successful rugby player and a newspaper editor. He is handsome, personable, and a good orator: a man to watch.

The hard realities of Afrikaner politics offering a pragmatic *verkrampte*

---

* One Nationalist commentator, at that time, called him "a failed clergyman, a failed journalist, and a failed politician."

(Mulder) as favorite and an ideological one (Treurnicht) as a serious contender for the succession is depressing news for *verligtheid* in the Republic. The *verligtes'* dilemma remains unresolved, for while they can publicize their views forcefully and influence individual politicians, they lack political weight within the party itself. The National party, although beset by doubt, is still a cohesive force; it still listens to the fundamentally conservative voices of the Afrikaner farmer, blue-collar worker, and middle-grade civil servant and responds appropriately; and it still puts unity before all else, a unity which it regards as synonymous with the salvation of the Afrikaner nation. Some *verligtes* are beginning to believe that they may have to break with the party if Vorster and his colleagues continue on their lackluster way to ruination. But the only real alternative at the moment is the liberal Progressive-Reform party, which for most *verligtes* is too radical a step. Another possibility for the *verligtes* is to try and take as many Nationalists as they can with them and form a new party, hopefully linking up with others in the center field, again not a very hopeful prospect. Other *verligtes*, and they are in the majority, feel there is no alternative but to continue proselytizing within the National party, using every method they can to build up *verligte* strength where it counts most. The appointment of Pik Botha —there are now four Bothas in the cabinet, all unrelated—as foreign minister has given them a little more hope. Botha, an experienced diplomat with a broad international perspective, proved himself a pugnacious and courageous political fighter when he defeated a *verkrampte* against the odds in the 1970 general election.

Vorster himself is a fitting symbol of his party. Politically, he is not moving much in either direction; he is determined to maintain unity in the rank and file, and, personally, he is not planning on going anywhere. He is a man of solid qualities but he is not an innovative thinker. Treurnicht's steady rise, fueled in part by his appeal to those who believe in the ideology of the separation of the races, is a measure of Vorster's failure to give a new lead that would attract the intellectuals and thinkers in the party. In this void, Treurnicht's voice is beginning to sound like a prophet's, a lilting, seductive voice for Afrikaners weaned on the Old Testament. But the tablets are the same: homelands (13 percent of the land) for the blacks, the rest for the whites. The implementation should be a little faster perhaps, but the scripture is written (the Great Doctor, Verwoerd himself, wrote it) and any significant deviation from it will lead to the destruction of the Afrikaner tribe. Fleur de Villiers, political correspondent of the Johannesburg *Sunday Times*, described to me the present immobility of Vorster's government in another way. "The cabinet," she said, "speaks with different accents, but it is the same language."

Vorster's own position is not in danger, and he is showing no sign of wanting to hand over to a younger man. Afrikaners have a history of divisiveness and also, paradoxically, of loyalty to their leaders, particularly if the man at their head displays strength and durability. Vorster, if nothing else, is a strong man. There is a belief that he would like to continue in office until at least September, 1979, assuming he wins the general election he has called for November 30, 1977, when he will have held power for thirteen years. There is, of course, no certainty that he will step down then, provided his health permits him to carry on. This is not a happy prospect for all those whites and blacks in South Africa who feel that the next three to five years may be the last chance they will have of restructuring their society and political system to accommodate reasonable, necessary, and, above all, peaceful changes.

While the government appears to be oblivious of the need for accommodation, it is busily accumulating even more power. Legislation over the last few years illustrates the steady flow of power to the executive: the Defence Act, obliging South African soldiers to fight anywhere in the world; the Parliamentary Internal Security Commission, a McCarthyite body set up to investigate suspect individuals and organizations; the Squatters Act, ordering landlords and local authorities to demolish squatters' homes and removing the occupant's right to appeal to the courts; legislation to enable the state to take a larger control of the country's commercial banks; the "SS" Act,* which increased the already draconian powers of the government in the field of individual liberties; and the Press Bill, which would have effectively censored the relatively free South African press (the bill has been shelved for a year but will be enacted if the press does not act "responsibly.")

The government may be considering a modification of the constitution in a move away from the present "Westminster" system—a figurehead president with an executive prime minister whose cabinet must be drawn from, and held responsible to, Parliament—toward an executive presidency of the American model. The purpose would be twofold: first, to concentrate still more power in the hands of the leader and, second, to enable the government to produce a more convincing system of consultation with nonwhite groups, especially the Coloureds, at the top level of government, yet still denying them representation in the white parliamentary process.

In September, 1976, a cabinet committee under P. W. Botha was appointed to investigate the possibilities of such a change. The idea for the committee came from the Erika Theron Commission, which dealt exhaustively with the future of the Coloured population of South Africa. The government rejected the commission's main recommendation that "provision be made for more satisfactory forms of direct representation and participation [for the Coloureds] in the decision-making processes" but showed more sympathy for the suggestion that the "existing Westminster form of

---

* Because of the sinister connotation of its initials, the title of this measure was changed from Promotion of *State Security* Act to Promotion of *Internal Security* Act. The South African government is often infelicitous in its choice of titles which abbreviate badly, *e.g.*, BOSS (Bureau for State Security), BAD (Bantu Administration and Development), PISCOM (Parliamentary Internal Security Commission).

government may well have to be changed."[6] It seems clear that the government has no intention of backtracking over power-sharing for the Coloureds or for any of the other nonwhite groups in the country. Coloureds and Indians at present consult with the government through the Cabinet Council, but *consultation* is one thing and *shared decision-making* another. (A few Nationalist politicians and commentators on the *verligte* side have suggested that Coloureds, Indians, and even urban blacks should eventually participate in the election of an executive president while remaining unrepresented in Parliament.)

There is, however, another interpretation of why the government may be interested in introducing an executive-style of presidency. André du Toit, the Afrikaner political scientist, points out that the Nationalists have no qualms about constitutional change when it enhances—or, at the very least, does not harm—their own electoral interests, as with the increase in the number of constituencies which favored the rural, largely Afrikaner vote and the lowering of the voting age to eighteen. Another academic, Professor Barry Dean, stresses that the South African legislature has increasingly abdicated its theoretical powers of control over the executive. He regards it as highly significant that Vorster did not recall Parliament during the urban riots but instead summoned a special meeting of the National party to give an account of his actions and sample the mood of his constituents. Dean suggests that Parliament has already been supplanted by the party as the link between the electorate and the executive and concludes that "the current proposals for a presidential-style executive, although changing the form of our constitution, will make little difference in practice."[7] The government's new constitutional plan, announced in August, 1977, and approved by the National party caucus, provides for the establishment of two or more parliaments, one for the Coloureds and one for the Indians, empowered to choose their own prime ministers and to pass laws for their own communities. The three parliaments—white, Coloured and Indian—will elect a joint cabinet council in which the whites will have an overall majority and choose an executive president. The plan offers nothing to the country's blacks.

Linked with the centralization of power is Vorster's determination to maintain Afrikaner unity. Despite the appeal of the Herstigte Nasionale party, the serried ranks of *verkramptheid*—the farmers, the white urban workers and their unions, the cultural organizations, and the churches—have no cause to be discontented with Vorster's government at the moment. It is important to remember that about a third of the total Afrikaner labor force is employed by the government in one capacity or another and that South Africa has the only substantial white working class in Africa, which, like the *pieds noirs* of colonial Algeria, is politically conservative and intensely jealous of its privileged position. Moreover, many of the divisive issues (rivalry between the Cape and Transvaal provinces, trade unionist versus *platteland* farmer, Bantu Department ideologue against *verligte* intellectual) often cut across each other and make a clear rift less likely. If, however, one issue became dominant and swamped all the others, then the party and the institution could be threatened. This is something Vorster will be at pains to avoid.

It would be wrong to ignore the effect on the Afrikaner of social and economic developments that have contributed to political change in other countries. Class divisions and generation gaps exist in Afrikanerdom as elsewhere and they may loosen some of the ethnic bonds as time goes by. No one can predict with precision what effect the new affluence will have on the Afrikaners or the impact of all the things that go with it, such as television (introduced in 1975); greater opportunities for travel abroad; changes in education (young Afrikaners are now taught to respect the "Bantu" and his ethnic identity); increased sexual permissiveness; the infiltration of international fashion, music, and lifestyles. The old image of the bearded Afrikaner farmer living a remote existence with his family, rifle, and Bible is no longer valid. Ninety percent of the Afrikaners are now urban dwellers; there are more Afrikaans than English universities; and a substantial middle class, well educated and affluent, is growing.

The generation gap between the young, middle-aged, and old appears to be one of degree rather than of quality. The older generation tends to be more puritanical and rigid in its values, while those in their forties show more receptivity to the trends and changes of the modern world. However, the idea that the young Afrikaners may become the spearhead of a reformist movement seems to be false. The liberal tradition in South Africa is still the almost exclusive preserve of the English-speaking universities, and even some of them have adopted a more conformist line as pressure on the whites has increased. In a detailed survey of young Afrikaner opinion, carried out in March and April, 1974, Laurence Schlemmer of Natal University found that among Afrikaner youth, "a broad and general enlightenment or *verligtheid* may not be emerging, but that the politics of colour may be swallowing the politics of culture." The survey also revealed "the almost complete rejection by all of the notion of financial sacrifice by whites for black development," giving a very clear indication of the limits of social conscience among white society. "Younger Afrikaners seem to be slightly more pragmatic than others but certainly no less discriminatory in their views on race policy," the survey found. It was also the youngest group that most strongly rejected the notion of a "common society" and expressed the least desire for more effective consultation between black and white leaders. Schlemmer concluded that the youth seem to "dread the prospect of black political influence on the same grounds as do older people" and that the Afrikaans newspapers' expectation of increasing *verligtheid* among the young Afrikaners might be unrealistic because the press "may very well be in unequal competition with the powerful socialising influence of the school system."[8]

Moving from the realm of what is to what could be is a hazardous journey for those who ponder, as well as for those who guide, the destiny of Africa's only white tribe. But there are numerous blueprints on the drawing boards of Afrikanerdom's political thinkers. The *verligtes* are the most industrious, though not the only, group active in this field, but they all share a certain coyness in exposing the details of their various proposals. The *verligtes* explain this by saying that their *verkramp* opponents would pounce on the most vulnerable parts and thus jeopardize the whole. Another problem is that separate development in its standard form has become such an article of faith with the National party in particular and with the Afrikaners in general that any major deviation from it smacks of treachery to the *volk,* especially when a proposal appears to be borrowing from the platforms of the English opposition parties, as some of the *verlig* federal schemes do. More radical solutions—a civilian dictatorship, a military takeover, partition, and so on—suggest either an even greater treachery or presuppose a greater crisis than is admitted to by the government. They are, nevertheless, also under consideration.

The basic *verligtheid* blueprint rejects majority rule as unacceptable ("one man, one vote, once only," the Afrikaners say), while agreeing that separate development as pursued by the government will never satisfy the Coloureds, Indians, and urban blacks. The logical consequence is constitutional decentralization resulting in more racial and regional autonomy with a federal or confederal arrangement at the center. *Verligtes* are studying all kinds of constitutional models, such as the Swiss, Malaysian, the Yugoslav, the Canadian, and the Turnhalle experiment in South-West Africa. The Bantustans are expected to be part of the new order, but the main concern of the *verligtes*—and this is where they are more realistic than their conservative opponents—is the future of the nonwhite groups in white South Africa. Piet Cillie, editor of *Die Burger,* using his "Dawie" nom de plume, put it this way in a November, 1976, article in his newspaper: "If there are nations or parts of nations in South Africa which have no real prospect of full citizenship in their own state, such prospect must be given them in a united state-structure with the whites. This is primarily not a demand of the outside world, but of our own principle of freedom."

Verligtes' hopes have been raised by Piet Koornhof, the minister of sport and immigration, who in June, 1977, advocated a Swiss-type of confederation for South Africa through which the "cultural pluralism" of the nation would be expressed. Koornhof is the leading *verligte* in the cabinet and was a member of P. W. Botha's committee on constitutional reform. But many privately feel that they may be forced to look beyond the Vorster era for meaningful solutions. One group is pinning its hopes on his probable successor, Connie Mulder, a surprising choice, it would seem, in that Mulder has always been regarded as a firm *verkrampte. Verligtes* are often accused of being unrealistic about the nature of power, and so this group asserts that it is only showing realism in expecting a Mulder succession, fully aware that the leadership of the National party cannot be secured by a man who has a liberal reputation. But they believe that Mulder, ten years younger than Vorster and less burdened by political traumas in his past, will prove to be more receptive to their ideas. The group has close contact with him in the Ministry of Information and feels that he is a man who combines an instinctive understanding of Afrikaner politics with a growing understanding of the need for radical change. As evidence of his gradual conversion, they point to his broadening comprehension of world affairs—after Pik Botha, he is the best-traveled man in the government—and his talk of "plural democracy," suggesting a more flexible approach to the problem of the Coloureds, Indians, and urban blacks. Mulder was the first cabinet minister to use the phrase "plural democracy" at the National party congress in September, 1976. He told the party that apartheid had "run its course and served its purpose"; the country should now look ahead to a "plural democracy."

Shortly after Mulder's speech, an analysis by a leading Afrikaner academic in the October 1, 1976, issue of the South African magazine *To the Point* had this to say:

> Experts have reason to believe that the newly-introduced
> Cabinet Council for the whites, Coloureds and Indian groups
> may be viewed as the beginning of a process of institutional
> evolution which will culminate in a sophisticated parlimentary
> system specially tailored to the needs of South Africa's multi-
> ethnic population structure. Democratic pluralism in this sense
> repesents a significant departure from the Westminster
> parliamentary system . . . . The fact that upper-echelon Nation-
> al Party leaders are already hinting at the need to have this
> model replaced by one more suited to the special needs of a
> plural society lends credence to the belief that Dr. Mulder's
> reference to plural democracy cannot be ignored as just
> another party-political gimmick. In the long-term, a plural
> democracy will evolve into a variant of the Swiss system. Cape
> National Party leader, P. W. Botha's reference to the merits of
> the Swiss canton system in his Port Elizabeth speech on 20th
> September [1976] thus assumes special significance when read
> in conjunction with Dr. Mulder's Pretoria speech.

Many of the government's critics dismissed "plural democracy" as another piece of separate development flimflam, a new wrapping for an old product; but Mulder's liberal Afrikaner friends believe it was meant seriously and, in a bleak political landscape, have read it as a sign of hope. Further, they believe that he possesses the same enlightened pragmatism and courage for tackling the racial conundrum that Vorster himself has displayed in handling the country's external problems. This is difficult to prove because, as Mulder's *verligte* supporters would be the first to admit, the man cannot show his enlightened colors—if indeed they exist—*until* he has become party leader. Up to that point, given the nature of the party rank and file, he must appear a staunch conservative, as he has always done, especially since the challenge to his favorite-son status is developing around the unbending Treurnicht on the right flank of the party.

Other *verligtes* believe that Mulder, or whoever succeeds Vorster, will be subject to the same immobilizing constraints, whatever pragmatism and courage they bring to the job and however much they try to shed their *ver-kramp* clothing, as long as the democratic system continues to function in its present form. Somewhat against their natural inclinations, their eyes are turning in the direction of more radical alternatives. *Verligtheid's* principal failing is its lack of power. Piet Koornhof is not a serious contender for the succession. Since political power is not going to be offered to the *verligtes* under the present parliamentary system, the system itself would have to be changed or suspended and replaced by a more authoritarian form of government that could then implement the necessary reforms. In practical terms, this would entail either a palace revolution by a reformist group within the party with military support or a straight military takeover with a reforming general at its head and underpinned by a *verligte* cabal. The conditions for making such moves would be a rapidly deteriorating situation inside South Africa, a neutral or hostile West, and a government in Pretoria that was either dithering or clinging to a reactionary course. A modernizing oligarchy of this kind, civil or military, would ride roughshod over the *verkrampte* die-hards in order to build a new order—almost certainly a federation—which would, they hope, appeal to some if not all the non-whites inside the country and to South Africa's friends outside. Opposition, whether from the white Right or the black Left, would be dealt with ruthlessly.

Political futurology is always tinged with fantasy. But it is a measure of the apprehension that a number of Afrikaners feel about the cul-de-sac Vorster has driven them into that they are thinking seriously about such a plan. They even have a name for it: the de Gaulle option, a reference to the French leader's recall to power in 1958 and his single-minded settlement of the Algerian crisis in the face of right-wing opposition. Willem de Klerk, editor of *Die Transvaaler* and perhaps the nearest the *verligtes* have to a leader outside the National party hierarchy, has warned that "responsible" people (he did not name them) had decided that only a dictatorship would solve the country's problems. The people that de Klerk was referring to probably include some of the military and members of the Bureau for State Security. There seems little doubt that the new military leadership—evenly balanced between Afrikaners and English-speakers—that has emerged since the retirements, promotions, and command reorganization in 1976 are in sympathy with *verlig* ideas and principles. They are mostly men in their midforties, oddly enough the most liberal age-group among the Afrikaners, a generation of soldiers brought up to think in political as well as military terms who have been taught that revolutionary war is 80 percent political and only 20 percent military. Many senior officers consider the Angola intervention a botched operation and blame the politicans, especially their own minister and senior members of the cabinet. Soweto, which blew up just as the army was launching a massive sweep operation against the South-West African People's Organization in Ovamboland on the Angolan border, felt like, in the words of one analyst, "a stab in the back." The military believe the police mishandled the black protests disastrously by being caught unawares without the proper riot-control equipment and training and then by overreacting in an unnecessarily brutal manner. According to the analyst quoted above, the army was better prepared both physically and temperamentally to cope with civil disorder than were the police at the time of the upheavals, and felt that it could have done a better job.

In the immediate wake of the Soweto riots, the military began to speak its mind with unusual candor. "If we lose the socio-economic struggle," General Gert Boshoff, the army chief of staff, said, "then we need not even bother to fight the military one." The commander of the South African air force, Lieutenant General R.D.H. Rogers, stressed that the government had to "do everything it could to win the hearts and minds of our own indigenous peoples." His views were echoed by Major General Neil Webster, head of the Citizen Force. "It would be a national tragedy," he said, "if the Defense Force had to suppress an uprising caused by a lack of mutual understanding and respect."[9] The tone is pure *verlig,* but it has to be remembered that the South African military, after a "political" phase under an Afrikaner chauvinist defense minister in the late 1950s and early 60s, now sees itself closer to its original British model, a modern, politically conscious, but not politically active military servant of a constitutional and legitimate government. Also, if it is true that colonels and above tend to be *verlig*-minded, then it is equally true that majors and below are generally *verkramp.*

Another "enlightened" power center appears to be the Bureau for State Security (BOSS). It has been known for some time that its director, General van den Bergh, holds realistic views on the future pattern of the Republic's relations with its neighbors and played a major part in crafting the government's live-and-let-live policy with Marxist Mozambique. One of Van den Bergh's *verlig* credentials is the venom which Albert Hertzog and the Herstigte Nasionale party pour on him as the CIA's "tool of liberalism." In an interview, Hertzog told me that the head of the Bureau of State Security did not understand the "natives" and was the instrument the United States used to persuade Vorster to adopt a more liberal line on racial matters. The famous October 25, 1976, *Newsweek* article "The View from BOSS," by Arnaud de Borchgrave, if it is taken at face value, gives a vivid and detailed account of the opinions of "key officials" in the organization. The Bureau of State Security's assessment, according to the article, is that a major realignment of black political forces inside South Africa is under way and that the government must "come to grips with reality and make drastic internal changes." This means nothing short of "a major constitutional revision" that would transform separate development.

> The revision, argue the leaders of BOSS, should provide for a Swiss-style cantonal system under a multi-racial federal or confederal umbrella. These cantons would be semi-autonomous—some black, some white and some mixed. The major difference between the black homelands and cantonal concepts is that under the cantonal arrangement blacks and whites would share a common citizenship and, therefore, a common national interest. The federal government would retain control over foreign

affairs and defence, but the cantons would be responsible for their own police and internal security. Once this transformation is accomplished, attempts by anyone to change it and impose black majority rule should be ruthlessly suppressed.

The government vehemently denied that this was indeed the "view from BOSS" and declared de Borchgrave a prohibited immigrant. There are many possible interpretations of the background to the article: that the ideas were deliberately "floated" as something Kissinger and the Americans, increasingly involved in southern African affairs, would like to hear; that the views expressed were the personal opinions of one individual in the organization and not those of either Van den Bergh or the Bureau of State Security as a whole (according to sources in South Africa, it seems probable that de Borchgrave spoke to Van den Bergh's deputy at the Pretoria headquarters); or that the general outline was laid out and then "hardened" in the writing. But the interesting point is that, "soft" or "hard," these attitudes dovetail almost perfectly with the standard *verlig* view that a federal solution recognizing the permanence of the urban blacks and sharing some power and decision-making with them is, for the Afrikaners, the only way out of their dilemma. I understand from a leading Afrikaner *verligte* that Van den Bergh personally favors a blueprint of this kind.

The main problem for the supporters of the de Gaulle option, apart from the enormity of traducing South Africa's long tradition of parliamentary government, is that there is no prince to play in their *Hamlet:* there is no South African de Gaulle. There are many *verligtes,* civilians and soldiers, who are highly regarded in Afrikaner society but none of sufficient standing at the moment to compete with a Vorster, a Mulder, a P.W. Botha, or a Treurnicht. General Magnus Malan, head of the Defence Force, has the reputation of being a good military leader, a soldier's soldier. But he is new to this job and, like the rest of the military, an unknown quantity in the political field. A left-wing military takeover, therefore, is no more likely than a right-wing one (the "Franco option"?) in the foreseeable future. The National party and the handful of men who control the central levers of power in Pretoria are too well entrenched to be ejected in a summary fashion. But palace—or, more accurately, party—revolutions are more plausible, though a *verligte* "Gaullist" bid for power might find itself blocked by a *verkrampte* "Salazar" oligarchy intent on doing the same thing.

Still within the realm of the future but not, I think, of fantasy, some Afrikaners are seriously considering an option which neither the *verligtes* nor the *verkramptes* of today condone: a radical partition of South Africa. Partition is not a new idea and, of course, it is already happening in a limited sense with the independence of the Bantustans such as the Transkei and Bophuthatswana. But there seems to be a new determination afoot in the opinion of careful Afrikaner-watchers like Jan van Eck, the editor of *Deurbraak.* In September, 1976, an elaborate partition plan, drawn up by the South African Bureau of Racial Affairs and said to be endorsed by some influential members of the Broederbond and the army, was unveiled to

1,200 Nationalist academics from the Afrikaans universities. The proposal scraps the concept of separating tribal groups, since the homelands would be joined in one or two black states, incorporating large chunks of present-day white South Africa that would include most of Natal, the northern Transvaal, and a portion of the Eastern Cape. The white "foot" within the black "horseshoe" would retain the Western Cape, most of the Orange Free State, and the southern and central Transvaal. (It will come as no surprise to the English that it is largely *their* areas of settlement that are destined to be sacrificed.) Again, the horseshoe and retreat-to-the-Cape theories are not new, but they are being pulled down from dusty shelves and brushed off with a new sense of urgency.

Behind the partitionists' maps there is ideology and a political rationale. The partitionists point out that the division of South Africa on a basis of 87 percent for the whites and 13 percent for the blacks is grossly unfair. This was done as long ago as 1936 by the Land Act, which produced the "measle map," a rash of small black spots dotted over the white body of the country. (See homelands map, centerfold.) They stress that the 1936 division—accomplished twelve years before the Nationalists came to power but not materially altered by them— was never intended as the basis for independent black states, is not fair, and will not work. They argue that crude white supremacy of the Herstigte Nasionale party variety is out of the question on both moral and practical grounds; that Vorster's slow implementation of an inequitable division of the land is equally wrong and increasingly untenable; that the *verlig* modifications will satisfy neither the whites nor the blacks and will not be implemented in time to make much difference anyway; and that the blacks' demand for majority rule is unacceptable. The logical conclusion is partition.

In September, 1975, a committee of twenty Afrikaner academics, including political scientists, sociologists, economists, and scientists, began work under the aegis of the South African Bureau of Racial Affairs in Pretoria. The basis of the partition plan is to consolidate, massively, the black homelands into two states separated by a white corridor running from the Transvaal to Durban in Natal. The black states would organize themselves whichever way they chose, in a loose or tight federation, linking up with Botswana, Lesotho, and Swaziland if a form of agreed association could be found. There would be a sustained drive to reduce the number of blacks in the white state and whites in the black states but whites who chose to stay, could, following the example of those who remained under black governments in Kenya, Zambia, and the Transkei. Industrial growth areas along the white corridor to Durban and in the Port Elizabeth-East London region (both eventually to be black-ruled cities according to the partition map I was shown) would provide the economic dynamo for the black states. More technology would be encouraged to reduce the black labor force on the white farms and in the white factories. The eventual aim in the reduced white state would be to whittle the number of resident Africans down to 4.5 million, about the same number as the total white population. Indians would have a self-governing enclave around Durban and the Coloureds a similar arrangement in three areas: Port Elizabeth, the Western Cape, and Witwatersrand in the Transvaal.

In keeping with the caution displayed by all Afrikaners engaged in plans that challenge the prevailing orthodoxy, the chairman of the South African Bureau of Racial Affairs Professor C.W.H. Boshoff, is reluctant to be more specific about the details of his partition plan. Like the Israelis with their peace maps for the Golan Heights and the West Bank, no partitioner in South Africa will fix a percentage for the quantity of land to be surrendered. However, one map I was shown in Pretoria in December, 1976, revealed huge tracts of territory, formerly white, turned over to the new black states, pushing up the black percentage to something nearer 40 percent of the total. The partitionists' strategy is to appeal both to the *verligtes* (on moral grounds) and to the *verkramptes* (no power-sharing of any kind with the blacks). They realize that the alternatives must be seen to be considerably starker than they are at present before their ideas will gain wider acceptance. They also believe that partition could only be implemented in a rational and effective manner under a dictatorial system of government, and they are not opposed to this. Their tactics are quiet, behind-the-scenes persuasion, aimed at the centers of Afrikaner power, rather different from the highly vocal and well-publicized *verlig* campaign. Boshoff told me he believes that as pressures build up, the white electorate and the government will see the inevitability of partition. Meanwhile, he and like-minded partitionists are spreading the concept at sophisticated levels in Afrikanerdom's many interlocking institutions. There has been some positive if muted response from the National party parliamentary caucus, and Gerrit Viljoen, head of the Broederbond, has talked of an eventual "retreat into a white homeland." Significantly, the partition lobbyists are making a determined effort to convert Andries Treurnicht. Boshoff and others admit that their concept is an extreme solution and will probably only become a viable proposition when the stark choices left to the Afrikaner are an unwinnable racial war, integration, or partition. When the storm that Vorster has warned is on its way finally strikes, the partitionists predict that the *volk* will trek back to the land it first settled and build a more viable and morally defensible citadel.

CHAPTER II

The Silenced Majority

Black power in South Africa is like Aladdin's genie. It suddenly pours out of the bottle, its head reaching up into the clouds and its feet straddling the land. Then it is gone again, the bottle capped, and life resumes its orderly rhythm. But a sense of unfulfillment for the blacks—and menace for the whites—lingers on and, with each new appearance, deepens. The bottle opened in 1960 with the passive resistance campaign against the pass laws; sixty-nine Africans were killed by the police at Sharpeville, and the stopper was rammed back in. In the early 1960s, the African nationalist movements turned to violence, were decapitated and banned. In 1973 the genie took on a different shape when the black workers of Durban sustained a lengthy strike that paralyzed the city. The government made concessions and the bottle was closed again. Then in June, 1976, the Soweto students' revolt began and swept through the country. Ruthless action by the police during the following six months quelled it at enormous human cost. The stopper is in once more, but no one can say with certainty how securely it is fastened.

Before looking at the urban heartland of black power, it might be worthwhile to examine its periphery, for, as with the whites, there are minority groups which influence, though rarely guide, the destiny of the majority. The Coloureds and the Indians are designated as separate racial entities by the South African government. The Coloureds are people of mixed race, a minority vis-a-vis both the whites and the blacks, yet people who share the language, religion, and culture of the former and the servitude of the latter. They are often called the "in-betweens" or the "brown Afrikaners," and economically, they are also in the middle, better off than the Africans but poorer than the whites. Most of the Coloured community lives in the Cape Province, where its position today is rather like that of the Negro in the American South before the civil rights era. Traditionally, the Coloureds have seen their future with the whites, fearing the possibility of black domination as much as the Afrikaners themselves. But there has been a significant change of view in recent years, both among the leadership and, even more markedly, among the youth. Before the National par-

29

ty came to power, the Coloureds were represented in the central parliament by a statutory number of white members. Apartheid, however, has progressively separated them from the whites, politically and physically, and driven them toward the blacks. The Coloureds, under separate development, have been given their own "brown" parliament, the Coloured Peoples Representative Council, which is an elected body with consultative and advisory functions, and they have their own political parties of which the Labour party is the largest. There is no Coloured homeland, and effective power remains with the Nationalist government in Pretoria.

In two successive elections—1969 and 1975—the Labour party under Sonny Leon has increasingly swung the Coloureds behind it* into a posture of confrontation with the government, culminating in the dismissal of Leon from the council's executive body in November, 1975. The Coloureds demand full citizenship in an integrated society. The government has rejected this demand, making it clear that the Coloureds will never regain their lost franchise nor be represented in the white parliament, "not now and not in the future" in the words of Connie Mulder, minister of information and the interior. The government's policy is inspired by its separate-development ideology and its fear that if the Coloureds were enfranchised in an integrated political system, they would join forces with the English-speaking opposition parties and oust the Nationalists. The creation of the Cabinet Council, a consultative body in which the government meets regularly with Coloured and Indian leaders to discuss common problems, has not satisfied the Coloured leadership, which continues to boycott the apartheid institutions designed for it.

For many years, the government managed to temporize over the Coloureds' future. In 1971 Vorster himself described his tactics with great candor. The relationship between white and Coloured political systems, he said, would be left to a future generation. The broad government view envisages a Coloured community that would continue to be closely interwoven with the white while developing its own institutions in a "parallel" manner but never moving in the direction of social and political integration.[1] The main flaw in the government's policy was that while separate development for the Africans led ultimately to Bantustan-style independence, "parallel development" for the Coloureds, as it came to be called, led nowhere.

The government would have left the Coloured's future on the shelf had it not been for their leaders' refusal to accept their fate and for the dissent that the issue caused inside the National party, particularly in the Cape Province where a strong liberal faction feels that the Coloureds have been given a raw deal and should be brought closer to the white community. The government was also under some pressure from the extreme, breakaway Herstigte Nasionale party, which advocated a geographical homeland for the Coloureds. So, in January, 1973, the government did what it

---

* The party won thirty-one seats out of forty in the 1975 poll.

often does when under pressure: it appointed a commission. Three and a
half years later, the Theron Commission, composed of whites and Coloureds and led by a liberal Afrikaner academic, Erika Theron, reported voluminously. The government accepted the bulk of the recommendations for social and economic reform but rejected the proposal that the laws forbidding marriage and sex across the color line should be repealed and the commission's main political recommendation that "satisfactory forms of direct Coloured representation in the various levels of government and decision-making bodies" should be provided. Even before the commission had presented its report, Vorster made it clear that there could be no concessions on the political issue. "I did not appoint the commission to work out a political policy for me," he told Parliament in April, 1976. He did, however, agree to appoint another commission, at cabinet level, to explore constitutional alternatives to the present Westminster system that might permit greater Coloured participation in government short of giving them the vote.

Sonny Leon's Labour party continues to defy the government, and the future of the community remains a source of often anguished controversy within the National party. The history of the Coloureds in their strange and unhappy no-man's-land has made them a complex people. There is no doubt that many of them still fear the blacks and would, if given an opportunity, side with the whites. But the whites have kept the door closed, while the blacks, especially the student-inspired black consciousness movement, have offered them an alternative in a new nonwhite alliance. The most striking example was the eruption of Coloured youth in the streets of Cape Town during the urban upheavals in 1976. Whites, for the first time, felt Coloured bitterness en masse, an experience that rocked the complacent belief that the Coloureds would automatically side with them in any showdown with the Africans. The effect of the riots has been to wring some concessions from the government, principally of an economic and social nature, and to radicalize Coloured youth, who now criticize their own leadership for not being tough enough with the government.

As a minority, do the Coloureds have anything to contribute to the power equation in South Africa? There are, I think, three critical factors. First, the government's failure to resolve satisfactorily the future of the Coloureds within the separate development blueprint leaves a gangrenous wound in the National party. The Coloured problem is one of the most divisive issues—some say *the* most divisive—among Afrikaners, who feel a historical responsibility and, increasingly perhaps, a future need for the Coloured people. A poll among 1,000 members of the Broederbond in the Cape in 1976 found that 73 percent were in favor of bringing the Coloureds back into the white political system. Another poll conducted by an Afrikaans university among 3,000 white voters found that no less than 83 percent believed that the white and Coloured communities should move closer together, although fewer supported parliamentary representation for the Coloureds. But the Transvaal branch of the party is more powerful, and no ground swell for reintegration exists there nor, for that matter, in Natal and the Orange Free State, demonstrating how the Coloured issue has split the party on geographical lines.

Second, the steady polarization of political forces, both black and white, in the country will probably edge the Coloureds closer to the blacks. Even before the Soweto riots, the Theron Commission reported that 24 percent of the Coloureds were willing to say that their future lay with the African majority, while 32 percent said they were uncertain. The youth, especially the students, are the strongest advocates of black consciousness, but it remains to be seen how far the Labour party will go, although there is no lack of clarity in its opposition to apartheid.

Part of the leadership is already fairly radical; but there is a deep reserve of conservatism within the community as a whole, and Sonny Leon finds himself on a political tightrope more often than in the past. David Curry, the deputy leader of the Labour party, put it this way in an interview: "While it is true that some Coloureds fear the blacks, the greatest binding factor in this complex heterogenous country is white oppression." Since that remark was made, two events—the urban riots and the government's rejection of the political reforms proposed by the Theron Commission—have illustrated the policies and determination of white authority. The government will undoubtedly seek to check the Coloured slide toward the black coalition by further economic and social reforms and perhaps by a new constitutional device to give the Coloureds a greater say in the handling of decisions that affect their own community, but there are indications that the too-little-too-late syndrome is already at work and that nothing short of an integrated political system and full citizenship rights will satisfy the increasingly politicized Coloureds.

The third factor in assessing the Coloureds' contribution to the power equation in South Africa is that the Coloureds have a potential pressure point in their physical concentration in the Cape Province and their high birthrate. Almost 90 percent of the Coloureds live in the Cape, a quarter of the total in Cape Town itself, outnumbering the whites of that city by three to two. The Coloured population stands at 2.4 million (9.3 percent of the total population of South Africa) as against 4.3 million whites (16.5 percent of the total). The Coloureds, however, are increasing at a faster rate than the whites, though slower than the Africans, and by the end of the century it is estimated that there will be 4.9 million Coloureds and 6.9 million whites.* The projection for the white population assumes a net immigration of 30,000 a year, which is the government's target, a rather optimistic figure under existing economic and political circumstances. If immigration does not occur at this rate, then it is conceivable that the Coloureds could outnumber the whites by the year 2010.

---

* The population figures are mid-1976 estimates produced by the Department of Statistics, Pretoria, 1976. The projections are based on probably the most accurate research done on South Africa's population growth by J. L. Sadie of the University of Stellenbosch and published by the Industrial Development Corporation of South Africa in 1973.

The sheer weight of the Coloured population in the Cape, and especially its concentration in the western part of the province, is bound to keep these problems alive in the National party. The apartheid system has given Coloureds priority over Africans in the Western Cape in an attempt to deter the latter from working and putting down roots there. In a situation where the whites find themselves in a growing confrontation with blacks, their need for allies, irrespective of color, will increase. The government, pressed by shortages of manpower, has already resurrected the Cape Corps, a Coloured infantry unit that was disbanded after the Nationalists took over in 1948, and the regiment has served on the Angolan border. A further consideration, no longer in the realm of fantasy, is the possibility of partition. The Cape Province, historically and as a fall-back position, is the Afrikaner's inner keep; yet within a generation there will be a separate and probably embittered people, almost as numerous as his own, sitting tight inside the castle walls. The geographical location of the Coloureds thus assumes a significance not only for the government but also for the blacks, who recognize the political value of the province and their own weakness in it. Both sides may try to woo the community as new alliances form and the struggle for power between Afrikaner and African intensifies. If David Curry is correct in his interpretation of the government's unbending attitude toward political rights for the Coloureds and their own refusal to accept anything less, then they may eventually throw in their lot with the forces of opposition whatever their hue.

The other nonwhite minority group is the Asian. This group is predominantly composed of Indians, the descendants of indentured laborers brought to Natal (where most Indians continue to live) in the second half of the nineteenth century. Numbering only 750,000 (3 percent of the total population), their role is likely to be minor on the national scene, although their potential for a regional impact on Natal cannot be discounted, especially in the event of partition. Wealthier than the Coloureds, permitted broader personal and commercial freedoms than the Africans, and more culturally exclusive than either, the Indians are not so much the in-betweens as the "almost theres." Indians, like the Coloureds, have no homeland but have shown a greater compliance with the government's separate development institutions. During 1977 their representative body, the Indian Council, will move from a partially to a fully elected status, and Indian leaders are participating in the government's new cabinet council, which permits them and the Coloureds to confer regularly with the prime minister and his colleagues in Pretoria. In his New Year's speech in 1977, Vorster said that he had fulfilled his promise to give the Indians a share in the decision-making process, suggesting that separate or parallel development for the Indian community had reached its final destination.

But there is also a tradition of opposition to white rule that goes back to Gandhi's time in South Africa before the First World War. In the 1950s, the Indian National Congress placed itself in the mainstream of African nationalism, and a number of prominent Indians have continued to take part in anti-apartheid activities in South Africa and abroad ever since. The black consciousness movement has attracted many Indian students and intellectuals, and the government's rigid policy of moving Indian traders out of designated white areas, regardless of how long they have been there, has aroused much resentment among a stratum of Indian society that does not normally have strong political views. However, the black riots in 1976, although not as widespread in Natal as elsewhere, resulted in some destruction of Indian property and exacerbated divisions within the community. Feeling continues to be divided about whether to support the Indian Council and play the government's separate-development game. In the opinion of government critic Fatima Meer, herself an Indian and now banned, "Indians see their ultimate security in South Africa to be in a racially integrated society in which they will have the same rights and the same dignity as other South Africans."[2] Whether or not they will be able to make more than a marginal contribution to that end is difficult to say. What is certain is that they dislike the present white dispensation and fear a black radical alternative.

Black power, when it is looked squarely in the eye, is African power. The latest government population statistics estimate that there were 18.6 million South African-born Africans and slightly more than 400,000 foreign blacks in the country in mid-1976—in all, 19 million. South African blacks currently form 71 percent of the total population; by the end of the century, their numbers will have risen to 37.3 million against the whites' 6.9 million, raising their proportion to 74 percent. By 2020 the blacks will have increased to 62.8 million to the whites' 9.2 million, 77 percent of the total.[3] The distribution of the African population around the country is less clear because of constant fluidity, some of it enforced by the government (such as the removals from white areas to the homelands), part of it the constant ebb and flow of legitimized migrant workers, and much of it the illegal but inexorable flood of impoverished rural peasantry into the cities, as impossible to monitor as it is to control. The generally accepted rule of thumb is that slightly less than half the African population, about 9 million, lives in the Bantustans and the other 9.6 million reside in the common area. Of the latter, some 5.6 million are probably in the cities, and the remaining 4 million live and work on the white farms.* The government has relentlessly

---

* According to the 1970 census, the number of Africans living in white rural areas was 3.65 million, about a quarter of the total black population at that time.

pursued its policy of removing "surplus" blacks from both urban and rural areas. One informed estimate puts the number of Africans forcibly resettled in the homelands at 2 million since 1968. The pass laws have been tightened in an effort to curb the influx from the countryside, and foreign migrant laborers have decreased from 500,000 in 1970 to slightly more than 400,000 in 1976.

Pinning down the physical location of the components of black power in South Africa is difficult enough; assessing their capacity and potential is even more hazardous. The mistiest area of all is the black peasantry who work on the white farms, a potential fifth column of vast proportions but very fragmented, highly dependent on the whites they work for, poorly educated, and somewhat of a mystery to black and white political leaders alike. For guerrilla infiltrators of the future, they are Mao Tse-tung's famous "sea," especially in the white farmlands close to South Africa's borders. For the government and their employers, they are docile, loyal, and ultimately expendable units of labor. It is government policy to modernize farming, making it more capital intensive, and to use where possible labor from neighboring Bantustans, thus reducing the numbers of Africans living permanently on white land. Living in a quasi-feudal condition, this black peasantry carries the greatest disabilities of all South Africa's peoples. Francis Wilson, the well-known economist of Cape Town University, has written:

> These black families are placed in a position of insecurity and
> total dependence upon the goodwill of their employers. A fami-
> ly expelled from a farm has no right to seek work in town and
> no claim upon a chief for land in a Bantustan. Legally such a
> family has no right to be anywhere at all.[4]

If the situation deteriorates into a violent conflict they will become helpless pawns as much of the Rhodesian and Ovambo peasantry have become further north. However, while there is peace and work, they are unlikely to be swept into the main current of black nationalism or consciousness or, indeed, to form part of the steady process of politicization that is going on in the townships, although there was a noticeable and possibly not unconnected ripple of rural arson during the period of black unrest in 1976. Nevertheless, while peace continues, so does the process of drift to the homelands and to the towns, the former encouraged by the government, the latter unavailingly discouraged. The problem for Pretoria is once again the remorseless march of demography and the dawning realization that the movement of people can never be controlled. Policy dictates a reduction of blacks on white land. A force greater than the government's ensures that for every illiterate and fundamentally harmless peasant who is dispatched to a homeland, there is another who will eventually turn up in a white man's city, where illiteracy and passivity may be exchanged for something damaging to the government's interest. As in most developing countries, the cities prove an irresistible magnet, whether there is work or not, and the government's strenuous attempts to check the flow have only been partially successful. It is generally accepted in South Africa that the official figures for the black townships are unrealistic: Soweto, for example, has an official population of 700,000, whereas in reality at least a million people live there, possibly many more.

The black labor force has a huge potential for putting pressure on the government by either threatening to withdraw its muscle or actually doing so. This is a most powerful lever because blacks fill 70 to 80 percent of the jobs in the country's farms and industries. It is also the lever least likely to be used for a number of reasons. Trade union leadership, vital for any mass action, has to operate under a blanket of restrictive laws and regulations. Black unions, although not illegal, are not registered in South Africa, which means that agreements they make with employers are not binding. Strikes by blacks are unlawful, and toward the end of 1976 the government began to emasculate the most active black unions by jailing and banning their leaders. Another constraint is the poor state of the economy and massive black unemployment, estimated variously at between one and two million, 10 to 20 percent of the total labor force. Since black unions are not registered and are therefore generally not recognized by employers, Africans who strike or stay away from work often find themselves victimized by their employers. It is perhaps significant that the most successful industrial action taken by black labor in South Africa's history, the 1973 Durban strikes, occurred at a time of economic boom and political stability. It is also significant that the government handled it with great delicacy, eschewing its usual confrontation tactics. In the post-Soweto era, however, diametrically opposite conditions exist because South Africa is now sunk in its worst recession since the 1930s and is passing through a period of political turbulence. Strikes, stoppages, and disputes occur continuously, but the power of labor remains seriously curbed by its inability to bargain collectively and by the growing army of unemployed waiting outside the factory gates.

On the periphery of black power but now in the zone of impressive numbers and clearly defined leadership are the Bantustans. There are ten of these, all based on the traditional homelands of South Africa's main tribal groups, covering about 13 percent of the country's land surface and inhabited by about nine million people. They represent the centerpiece of the government's separate-development concept. The theory is that the homelands will become independent mini-states, based on the ethos of the single tribe, where all blacks will express themselves politically and where all will have the right of "return," as Jews of the Diaspora do in Israel, if they so choose. The practical problems of implementing this policy—homeland fragmentation, inadequate land and resources for the existing populations, the refusal of some homeland leaders to take independence and of most urban blacks to accept citizenship, to name but a few—have not deflected

the government from its course. At its best, the homeland strategy can be
seen as a means of accelerating much-needed development of the neglected black rural areas and providing a secure base for each of the tribal units without which, many South Africans believe, they would be in constant fear of each other's aggressive desires to dominate. At its worst, it is a strategy designed to dump the country's unwanted blacks, depriving them and those who remain of any share in the nation's wealth—except through the sale of their labor—so that undiluted white control may continue over the remaining 87 percent of the country.

The Bantustan idea emerged piecemeal in the early days of the Nationalist government but was given coherence and purpose by Hendrik Verwoerd in the late 1950s and early 60s. With the frankness that often characterizes Afrikaner leaders, he admitted that he had agreed to independence for the Bantustans because outside presssures on South Africa demanded that the Africans should be given something, naked white supremacy no longer being possible. The government, pursuing the strategy with growing energy, has achieved some success and struck a chord of common interest with several homeland leaders. Chief Kaiser Matanzima of the Transkei agreed to independence, and the Transkei became independent on October 26, 1976. No government, outside Pretoria, has recognized it, but the Transkei, still in three separate pieces, although larger and more viable than several recognized members of the United Nations, is a separate entity. Matanzima has thus taken about 3 million Xhosas out of the political arena but left over a million in white South Africa. The status of the latter is disputed: Matanzima says they are the responsibility of Pretoria, while the government replies they are Transkei citizens. In practice, they are being slowly compelled, through the administrative process, to accept Transkei citizenship.

The centrifugal forces that impelled Matanzima are at work on the other homeland leaders. Chief Lucas Mangope of Bophuthatswana has agreed to independence on December 6, 1977, even though his territory is scattered in six pieces over three provinces, from the central Transvaal to the northeastern Cape to the eastern Orange Free State. Lebowa in the northern Transvaal is another possible candidate for independence, and others may follow regardless of the government's failure to consolidate them and in the teeth of the Organization of African Unity's hostility and general international ostracism. Most of the homeland leaders are tribal chiefs of a conservative nature who came to the conclusion some time ago that there was no future in trying to fight the government's Bantustan plan and that the only option they had was to work within the system and use the power base Pretoria provided, limited though it might be, to improve the lot of their people. Their interests have always tended to be local and the majority of the Bantustan leaders have made it clear that they cannot be held responsible for blacks who have settled, and wish to remain, in the white cities. The government has held out strong financial and other inducements to them to move faster along the road to independence. For example, in the period before the Transkei's independence, the government increased its budget for the territory from $11 million (1975-76) to $41 million (1976-77). The feeling in Pretoria is that if the Transkei experiment is seen to be a success, the other Bantustans will follow suit. All of them are heavily dependent on the central government's purse and the earnings of their migrant citizens working in the Republic, which constitute the life blood of their national incomes. More than two-thirds of the Transkei's budget is funded by Pretoria and 70 percent of that territory's gross national income is derived from its migrant workers. The other Bantustans are even more dependent; for example, although 55 percent of the Ciskei's population lives in the homeland, only 5 percent earn their living there.

The most interesting and controversial figure among the homeland rulers is Chief Gatsha Buthelezi, the leader of the Zulus. Buthelezi has consistently opposed the government from his base in the KwaZulu Bantustan, another fragmented and impoverished rural area situated in Natal. He is strongly opposed to independence for the Bantustans; he insists that the homelands do not now, and can never satisfy the political aspirations of the urban blacks; that the black people of South Africa belong to the whole country and have a single destiny; and, in the most explicit clarification of his position yet, he called in March, 1976, for majority rule in a united South Africa. There is no doubt that Buthelezi is a thorn in the government's flesh, especially in its right, *verkrampte* flank. The government, however, would be reluctant to muzzle him because his legitimacy and Bantustan platform are the creation, indeed the showpiece, of the separate-development doctrine. Buthelezi, a subtle politician with genuine charisma, has used his base astutely, fighting off attempts to depose him locally, speaking as a *KwaZulu* leader but on *national* stages (every year he makes a major speech in Soweto and other urban areas) and traveling abroad drumming up support for his cause.

By far the most politically engaged of the homeland leaders, Buthelezi is playing a complex and difficult game. He aspires to a national role in the black leadership but has chosen to retain his regional base for the time being. To a certain extent, he conforms to the broad outlines of government policy. He is opposed to violence as a means of change, he encourages local and foreign investment in the homelands, and his constituency is principally, though not exclusively, Zulu—a fact which dovetails with the government's notions of ethnicity and tribal nationalism. But he is an unrelenting and eloquent critic of apartheid. Criticizing the independence of the Transkei, which he vainly tried to prevent, he said: "This act denies to the urban blacks the possibility of citizenship amid the plenty their toil and sweat has created. It offers the rural blacks the possibility of citizenship amidst the poverty their toil cannot prevent. Statelessness is the citizenship of the exploited." And on the critical issue of land apportionment and consolidation, he commented in a speech to the Inkatha movement on July 8, 1976: "The government's claim to be making a just distribution of territories between black and white is a deceitful metaphor, and its literal meaning can be driven home by [our] claiming "a share" in the industrial heartland."

He tried to build a common front among the Bantustan leadership,

but this effort fell apart when Mantanzima decided to opt for independence. In an interview in Zululand in April, 1976, Buthelezi told me that he
could only count on the support of two other leaders—Hudson Ntsanwisi
of Gazankulu and Cedric Phatudi of Lebowa—to stand firm. Since then,
there have been signs that Phatudi is breaking ranks, an indication of the
government's success in tempting others to follow the Transkei's primrose
path. More significant, however, has been Buthelezi's determination to
strengthen his own base with the formation of Inkatha or, to give it its full
name, the National Cultural Liberation Movement. This is primarily a Zulu
organization, which has its base in Zululand but reaches out into the urban
areas. It is well-organized, well-funded, and, with 70,000 members, growing
rapidly; its overt aims are cultural, but there is no mistaking its political col-
oration. Buthelezi has also launched a new national newspaper in English
—he already has the support of the Zulu newpaper in Durban—called *The
Nation*, owned by Inkatha, which has given itself the task of "furthering
black solidarity in the national struggle for liberation." Some observers in
South Africa regard Inkatha, and all that goes with it, as Buthelezi's standby
platform, the one he will leap onto when he jumps—or is pushed by the
government—off his KwaZulu base. Meanwhile, he is reaching out to the
center while keeping his feet firmly on the rim of black politics.

For several years Buthelezi has been calling for a national convention
to hammer out a new black strategy, but without success. Since the urban
riots, in which he effectively mediated between the students and the hostel
workers—Zulus and others—when they clashed bloodily in Soweto, he has
altered his tactics and joined the Black Unity Front, a loose coalition of his
own Inkatha movement, some of the Bantustan rulers, members of the urban Bantu councils in the townships and other prominent moderate black
leaders. He has also been in contact with the all-white Progressive-Reform
party, probing the multiracial middle ground of South African politics and
sundering a hitherto sacrosanct apartheid barrier.*

Buthelezi's bid for the center—moderate black and liberal white—
using his government-provided homeland base has alienated the black
Left. The exiled nationalist movements assert that he has made apartheid
respectable abroad and criticize him for his decision to encourage foreign
investment in the Bantustans. They accuse him of pursuing the "politics of
development" instead of the "politics of liberation." Buthelezi defends himself by saying that the homelands are rural slums that should have been
developed years ago and that improving the lot of the Africans who live in
them will strengthen rather than weaken the black cause. Defenders of
Buthelezi say he is fighting apartheid with apartheid. The black Left replies
that Pretoria has given him an empty gun.

One of the criticisms leveled against Buthelezi by black nationalists in
South Africa—by people like Robert Sobukwe, the banned Pan-Africanist
Congress leader, and Steven Biko, the former president of the South Afri-

---

* There is a law in South Africa prohibiting the formation of political parties
across the color line. It is called the Political Interference Act.

can Students Organisation, who died in prison in September, 1977—is that the Zulu leader is saying the right thing but from the wrong platform. They assert that he is missing—or has already missed—the boat by clinging to the base provided by the apartheid system, and that he should have followed Sonny Leon's example by rejecting the government's institutions. A number of more middle-of-the-road Africans, in the wake of the Soweto riots, were hoping that he would abandon his officially sanctioned position in KwaZulu and assume a national role. Buthelezi, however, clearly believes that the time is not ripe for such a move and that his stepping out of the Bantustan framework now would merely provide Vorster with the opportunity he has long sought to silence him. The radicals grant that Buthelezi has exceptional powers of leadership and that he is a man of great charm, intelligence, and sincerity. But they think he is too egotistical and ultrasensitive to criticism to cope with the problems of a national coalition of black forces, although they say that since the Soweto riots he has subtly changed his rhetoric to match the more radical atmosphere of the times.

The black Left's most serious charge against the Zulu leader is that he is just that, a Zulu leader. They regard with alarm his efforts to build a strong tribal base, with the Inkatha movement, among South Africa's most numerous, homogeneous, and warriorlike tribe.* In an interview, Robert Sobukwe made a distinction between Matanzima's (and other homeland leaders') *geographical* tribalism, which consolidates the rural population but stops there, and Buthelezi's *political* tribalism, which, through Inkatha and other means, reaches out to weld tribal support in both rural and urban constituencies, thus weakening attempts to achieve unity among urban blacks of different backgrounds. There is no doubt in Sobukwe's mind which is the more harmful to the black nationalist cause.

Buthelezi denies vehemently that he is a Zulu nationalist and says Inkatha is open to all, regardless of tribal background. There is no accurate way of testing his non-Zulu support in the country, although he usually draws large crowds representing all tribes when he speaks in Soweto or other black townships. The trouble is that while he talks like a black South African nationalist and certainly acts like one, his power base is still demonstrably the Zulu homeland. Also, the Zulus' history of black imperialism and the government's policy of keeping the tribes as separate as possible—in the townships, living areas, education, trading, etc. are administered on tribal lines—have helped to maintain inherent tribal divisions. Finally, the Transkei's independence has removed a large number of Xhosas from the central arena, leaving the Zulus by far the most numerous single tribe in the Republic and strengthening fears of Zulu "domination."

Many black radicals feel that Buthelezi's time is already past and that the revolutionary dynamic that expressed itself during the six months of continual unrest in 1976 will sweep him back onto the periphery of South

---

* The main tribes in the Republic are: Zulus (5 million); Xhosas (4.9 million); Tswanas (2.1 million); Bapedi (2 million); and Sothos (1.7 million). These are mid-1976 estimates from the Department of Statistics, Pretoria, 1976.

African politics. However, they view with some concern his involvement with the Black Unity Front—the coalition of conservative forces—and his contacts with the white liberal Progressive-Reform party, which, though small, is gathering more support. The black Left does not consider the political weight of these forces very significant at the moment. But it is worried about the strategy behind moves that it regards as detrimental to the cohesiveness of black power. Some nationalist leaders think Buthelezi may be setting himself up for "stoogedom," the man to whom the whites will eventually turn when, under the threat of losing the whole loaf, they will offer him half: a South African Kapuuo. (Ironically, the white Right, and that includes the bulk of the National party, is equally appalled at what to it looks like an attempt at resurrecting the old British imperial demon of an English-African alliance against the Afrikaner.) Buthelezi refutes this analysis in the strongest terms, stressing that he maintains a productive dialogue with representatives of the banned African nationalist movements outside South Africa and asserting his role as a spokesman for all blacks, whatever their tribe, in the Republic.

Leaving aside Buthelezi's unique role for the moment, the crucial question about the Bantustans is what effect will they have on the balance of power in the Republic, for whatever one's ideological position may be, there is no denying that ten rural polarities of power of varying strengths exist, that they are the homes of almost half of the country's black population, that they may grow larger and stronger, and that several more may accept Pretoria's gilded offer of independence, thus creating a small, messy, but de facto partition of South Africa. Will the Bantustans strengthen or weaken black power? There appear to be three possibilities: 1) they will make a contribution to the coalition of black forces by using their autonomy (or independence) to wring concessions out of Pretoria; 2) they will do nothing of the kind and instead will cooperate fully with the government, thus strengthening its hand against the urban blacks; or 3) the homelands will never leave the drawing board and become increasingly irrelevant as the struggle intensifies, their only significance being the weakness which their independence will have brought to the government's perimeter defenses.

    None of the Bantustans will in the foreseeable future be able to ignore their almost total economic and geographic dependence on the Republic. The Transkei, because of its size, relative homogeneity, access to the sea, and bountiful rainfall, is the best placed to assert its independence. Yet it will remain dependent on South Africa for the bulk of its budgetary funds, for the greater part of its national income, for development capital, for the training and supplying of its army and police, for technical assistance of all kinds. And if the Transkei is doomed to the status of a client state, the other Bantustans are infinitely worse off. The examples of Botswana, Lesotho, and Swaziland, independent for more than a decade but still locked into the South African economy and still "captive" in the sense of having their political options severely curtailed by that dependence, give some idea of the straitjacket constraining the independent Bantustans of the future.

Another factor suggesting restraint toward Pretoria is the nature of the Bantustan leadership. With the exception of Buthelezi of KwaZulu and Ntsanwisi of Gazankulu, the homeland rulers are conservative tribal figures whose ambitions are limited to their rural fiefs. They know that the resources they need are in Pretoria's dispensation; they do not trust each other and often compete for government funds and for the private capital which is channeled through the government-run Bantu development corporations. Given the existing state of international frigidity, the Bantustan leaders know they are unlikely to receive much outside help. They are also suspicious of their tribal kith and kin in the neighboring states of Botswana, Lesotho, and Swaziland, although the South African government would welcome mergers between contiguous areas, such as Bophuthatswana with Botswana, the Basotho Qwaqwa with Lesotho, the Swazi homeland with Swaziland, and so on. Moreover, the experience of Africa in recent years shows that once power is established in a state, whatever its true legitimacy, it digs deep roots and defends itself tenaciously. Finally, the Bantustan policy has already had a divisive effect on black nationalism in South Africa, and there is little reason to doubt that as the experiment picks up momentum, the confusion it sows will continue to grow. Knowledge Guzana, leader of one of the opposition parties in the Transkei and a resolute opponent of homeland independence, put it this way to me in an interview: "Mr. Vorster is trying to reverse modern trends in Africa. In the same breath he tells us to become urbanized and yet remain tribalized, to have a democratic parliament and then to pack it with chiefs. What does he expect from all this? A hybrid has no progeny."

This, of course, is precisely the government's aim. The tactics are familiar enough to any student of African colonial history. Pretoria is relying on the traditional power of tribal chiefs, which is still considerable in the rural areas, and on the traditional animosities among the tribes themselves, which remain strong despite the urbanization process and common opposition to the white man. The British did it in their colonies; Ian Smith tried it, without too much success, in Rhodesia; and the South Africans are also doing it in South-West Africa. It is significant that the constitutions of the Bantustans are weighted heavily in favor of the traditional leadership. Half the seats in the Transkei parliament are reserved for the government-appointed and government-paid chiefs. The same is true for Bophuthatswana and the other homelands.

There is a democratic sauce spread over the top of homeland governments, but the dish itself is fundamentally authoritarian. In the Transkei's first elections in 1963, Matanzima lost the popular vote and only became the territory's chief minister by virtue of the support of the chiefs. Later, however, he won a clear majority of the elected representatives in the next three elections, although in the one immediately preceding independence he locked up the leaders of the main opposition party before the poll took place. But there is a variation in South Africa's policy: it is less divide and rule than divide and dump. The government has no desire to hold onto the homelands—nor any longer to South-West Africa for that matter—because its main purpose is to reduce the black population as much as it can in the central "white homeland" and tie what is left with a tribal knot to each of the Bantustans. A secondary goal is to ensure that the black homelands remain unrestrictive suppliers of labor and do not harbor the enemies of the Republic.

It is clear that Pretoria's leverage with the Bantustans is formidable, but do the Bantustans themselves have any leverage? The homeland leaders do hold a few cards, though none of them are aces. For separate development to move ahead the government needs their cooperation in a number of ways. Accepting or rejecting independence is the Bantustan leader's strongest card. The common Bantustan "rejection" front has been broken, and those who have done the breaking have thrown away another card with it, the one that demanded consolidation *before* independence. With independence and without consolidation, a homeland leader has little room to maneuver. He can continue to deny responsibility for his tribal cousins who elect to remain in South Africa, as Matanzima has done; he can seek foreign recognition and assistance—Pretoria would cheerfully endorse that appeal; or he can assert his independence by critical speeches and even verbal threats against his former masters.

On paper, the Bantustans possess leverage through the vast army of citizen-workers who are domiciled there but employed on contract in the Republic. If these workers could suddenly be withdrawn, as Malawi pulled out its 60,000 miners at a stroke after an air crash killed 74 of them in April, 1974, then Pretoria would have reason to be worried. But the homelands are far more economically beholden to South Africa than Malawi is and find themselves rather in the position of impoverished Lesotho, which, though frequently on bad terms with the South African government, has never dared to threaten a move of this kind. A carefully coordinated boycott by the largest Bantustans would constitute a serious threat; but as failed attempts at coordination between Botswana, Lesotho, and Swaziland have shown, where even a joint university soon broke up, this is extremely unlikely. And then there is always the chance that the South Africans might call their bluff, leaving tens of thousands of workers unemployed, clamoring for jobs or land that simply are not available. The "labor lever" exists, but it is hard to conceive of a situation in which it could be pulled. For a long time to come, the Bantustans' livelihood will be slavishly dependent on the export of their muscle.

Some supporters of the Bantustans talk bravely of twisting the lion's tail in Pretoria by opening their doors to the black nationalist movements and providing refuge for political exiles from the Republic. This is a logical collorary to the notion that the South African government has unwittingly created a series of mini-Frankensteins that it will not be able to control or, to change the metaphor, planted a number of time bombs within its borders that will go off at inconvenient intervals. Again, in theory, places like the Transkei, with 200 miles of coastline and a common border with independent Lesotho, should have the option of adopting a more militant approach. But, under scrutiny, the theory disintegrates. The Bantustan leaders, by and large, accepted the system because they came to the conclusion that they could not fight it. They perservered to the point of independence and were bitterly attacked by the black nationalists as traitors, as "self-seeking salesmen of their countrymen's birthright." Their major interest is to hold what they have and improve and enlarge it as and when they can. They need Pretoria more than they need the African National Congress or the Pan-Africanist Congress. They may be prepared to pay lip service to the concept of African nationalism and to thumb their noses at their white neighbor in small ways as, for example, the Transkei has done by abolishing the Republic's race laws. But they are not going to turn their overcrowded rural islands into launching pads of revolution. Quite apart from Pretoria's certain interdiction, they know that their own leadership would be challenged if they permitted a build-up of armed radical forces within their borders. This is not to say that some of the Bantustan rulers are lifeless puppets who dance every time a string is pulled in Pretoria. Matanzima, for example is a stubborn, inscrutable man and his government includes a few former active nationalists. There is talk of African National Congress and Pan-Africanist Congress opening in Umtata, the capital, and refugees from the Republic may find a safe haven in the Transkei. But he has made it clear that he intends to remain Pretoria's friend. He told the Transkei legislative assembly in 1975: "Our army, which South Africa will be asked to train, will stand side by side the Republic's." A small branch of the Bureau for State Security was loaned to him at the time of independence, just to keep an eye on things perhaps.

It is difficult to envisage the Bantustans contributing to black power under their present conservative governments. Coups, of course, could occur bringing radicals to power, but these are unlikely under South Africa's protective shield. What part, if any, are they likely to play in the struggle ahead? The homelands are already Pretoria's black auxiliaries.* Some of them are too small to be relevant. Basotho Qwaqwa, for instance, reputedly the homeland of 1.7 million Sotho, although only 8 percent of them actually live there, is a mere 120,000 acres; its leader calls it derisively "my farm": Bantu without a Stan. Many black nationalists consider that events both inside South Africa and on its borders are moving fast enough to make the Bantustans irrelevant regardless of how quickly or how successfully the government's policy is implemented. They contend that the vortex of the struggle in the heartland of South Africa will suck these detached fragments back in. Robert Sobukwe, the Pan-Africanist Congress leader, is

---

* There are plenty of historical precedents for Afrikaner-African alliances. The final defeat of the Zulu leader Dingaan in the nineteenth century came not at Blood River but at the hands of another group of Zulus which had allied itself with the Boers.

convinced that the homelands will not be able to impede the nationalist cause. He stresses that they have many links with the mainstream of South African political life, such as their opposition parties, their workers, and their close identification with Pretoria, which will prevent them from establishing the kind of independent identity that Botswana, Lesotho, and Swaziland have achieved despite their overwhelming economic dependence on the Republic. Sobukwe also believes that homeland independence—he is under no illusions that others will not follow the Transkei's example—will loosen South Africa's borders because their security forces will not be as efficient, or perhaps as willing, to check African National Congress or Pan-Africanist Congress activity. An illustration of the interrelation of events in urban areas and the homelands came with the Soweto riots, which had a severe dampening effect on international recognition for the Transkei.

Sobukwe, like other realists in South Africa, does not deny that the Bantustan leaders have a large measure of popular support within their territories and that the common people who live in places like the Transkei welcome independence for the freedom, dignity, and small economic benefits that it brings to them as individuals. Transkei citizens are now free of the endless regulations and restrictions that apartheid imposed on their daily lives; they have a place that they can call their home, a place where they can move freely, live, eat, drink, and trade where they like. They also have a government that can issue them passports to go abroad, a government that has already abolished the detested "Bantu" system of education and introduced English as the teaching medium in all its schools, and a government that can stand up for them when they are working for the white man in the Republic. As long as the Bantustan governments continue to bring some benefits and some degree of protection to their rural peasantry and their migrant workers, they are likely to retain their allegiance even though they tend to govern autocratically and at times repressively. And in doing so, they will aid and abet Pretoria's grand strategy for separating and containing black pressures. But that seems to be the limit of the homelands' power. The rest of the black millions in the white man's cities, farms, factories, mines, kitchens, and gardens, although technically as much their citizens as their own peasantry, will be beyond their control. The South African government will have to face those blacks alone.

The black students' revolt, which began with the Soweto demonstration on June 16, 1976, and continued sputtering angrily and bloodily around the country for the next six months, was the most unexpected and threatening manifestation of black power that South Africa had ever seen. The genie burst out of the bottle and took the government, especially the police, by surprise. The nature of the upheaval revealed new tactics for which the government had no other response than minor concessions or massive repression. The spontaneity of the demonstrations, the widespread support they received, including the participation of the Coloureds in Cape Town, and, above all, the fearlessness the demonstrators displayed facing the gun shook the government and many of its white supporters. Having crushed the African nationalist organizations in the 1960s, the security services seem to have thought that no new form of mass protest could take place without their knowing in advance. But it was the *lack* of organization on the part of the students that both defeated the police and has since proved a source of puzzlement. For, as Colin Legum, assistant editor of the London *Observer*, has pointed out, "Anything that is organised in South Africa is affected; and anything that's effective is spontaneous." The countrywide extent of the unrest suggested that the tinder was dry and the bravery of the thousands who faced the bullets that a new mood was alive among the Republic's black youth.

The spirit that sustained the revolt can be attributed largely to the spread of black consciousness in South Africa, encouraged notably by the South African Students Organisation and the Black Peoples Convention, which, ironically, grew out of the government's new all-black universities. Black consciousness defines a black man as anyone who is not white and who is discriminated against because of color. In the South African context, the definition embraces all Africans, the Coloureds, and the Indians and is at the opposite pole from the government's finely honed theories of separate ethnic identity.* Steven Biko, the first president of the South African Students Organisation and an inspirational force in the movement, stressed that black consciousness is primarily a search for the black man's identity and not a racist ideology. South African black consciousness drew some of its generating force from the American black movements of the 1960s and from African nationalist leaders to the north, but Biko insisted that it is not slavishly following anyone. It rejects equally the white liberal as paternalistic and the white reactionary as racist. It stresses traditional African values of communalism but allows scope for enterprise. Africans are seen as fundamentally Christian, although some of the Bible's racial stereotyping needs to be reinterpreted. In Africa, Julius Nyerere's socialist experiment in Tanzania is probably the nearest to the black consciousness movement's ideal model, although allowance has to be made for the complex nature of the South African economy.

The South African Students Organisation, founded in December, 1968, was the organizational core of the movement. It spawned a number of other groups, not all of them overtly political but all dedicated to redefin-

---

* The South African Students Organisation, in its second General Students Council Policy Manifesto, produced in July, 1971, defined black people as "those who are by law or tradition, politically, economically and socially discriminated against as a group in South African society and identifying themselves as a unit in the struggle towards the realisation of their aspirations."

ing the black man's identity in a country where they felt it had been submerged too long by the white man's stereotypes. The new organizations included trades unionists, priests, actors, social workers, and teachers, and their activities have embraced theological conventions, community programs, and theater groups. In July, 1972, the Black Peoples Convention was formed as a senior partner to the South African Students Organisation and, increasingly, acts as an umbrella organization for the whole black consciousness movement. One of the interesting things about the consciousness phenomenon is that it began at a time when the South African government was complacent and secure and when the future of African nationalism looked bleak in the whole of southern Africa. Another point is that by raising the level of consciousness of the black man's identity, the movement is also heightening his political awareness, since the two are inseparable in South African society. The degree of politicization among young blacks became more clearly evident when the Portuguese began to withdraw from their African colonies. The South African government then began to react more harshly to the movement, and the familiar pattern of repression followed, resulting in the arrest, imprisonment, or banning of many of the movement's leaders. A trial of nine organizers, which lasted over two years and ended in December, 1976, was technically concerned with a pro-Frelimo (Mozambique liberation front) rally that they had organized in September, 1974, but it turned out to be more a judgment of black consciousness than of treason, conspiracy, or terrorism. The accused were found guilty of "endangering the maintenance of law and order" and were sentenced to terms of five to six years' imprisonment. The trial is important because it established that black consciousness, as advanced by the South African Students Organisation-Black Peoples Convention leadership, is unlawful in South Africa.

The government, however, has not yet banned the organizations as it did the nationalist movements, though it may act if it finds that selective arrests, harassment, and banning of individual militants fail to serve as an effective muffler. The township upheavals, orchestrated by high school student groups like the Soweto Students Representative Council—a sort of junior Students Organisation—showed both the blacks and the government that a plethora of organizations and a diffuse leadership present a more elusive target than a hierarchically structured organization of the traditional nationalist type. A measure of the black consciousness movement's success is this hydra-headed quality, which so far has enabled it to survive against the government's formidable informer-ridden security network.

Dedicated to working outside the system, the young blacks face three major problems in the future. The first is the unrelenting hostitily and vigilance of the state, which can be counted on to keep up the pressure against any committed organization or individual. The police, discredited badly by their unpreparedness and then their overreaction, will adopt more sophisticated methods—they are already doing this with riot control—and spare no effort to crush the "agitators." The government, meanwhile, will continue its removal program, eradicating "black spots" and packing off surplus labor to the homelands. Africans who trace their origin to homelands that have become independent will be compelled, through the bureaucratic process, to become citizens of those territories whether they like it or not.

Second, the cost in lives of opposing the government, plus the harsh economic effects of the recession, are likely to take their toll of the foot soldiers of black power. The statistics, listed by a reputable South African journalist, after six months of violence in 1976 read as follows: 360 blacks killed (a conservative figure); 2,915 brought to court; 1,381 convicted, of whom 927 were juveniles under eighteen years of age; 528 flogged; and 697 detained without charge or trial under the Internal Security Act.[5] (South Africa's Institute of Race Relations named 558 Africans and Coloureds who had been killed in the riots.) There are already indications that the students are adopting new tactics to reduce such heavy tolls: for example, consumer boycotts of selected traders have proved more effective, though less dramatic, than mass stay-aways. But the government has not been idle either. Some of its concessions, such as more money for black education, home ownership, electrification of Soweto, and greater self-governing powers for the urban Bantu councils (UBCs)—dubbed the Useless Boys Clubs by the townships' youth—are aimed at undermining support for the movement. Keeping a revolutionary momentum going when the revolution has not taken off is a hard, some would say impossible, task. Previous black eruptions petered out quickly, but, for the black youth at least, there has been a qualitative change since June 16, 1976. "We are no longer afraid, and we feel that time is on our side" might sum it up.

The third problem, to their mind, is as serious as the other two. It is the black coalition of conservative forces led by Gatsha Buthelezi. The consciousness movement criticizes Buthelezi for having, they claim, made apartheid "respectable" by operating freely within it, and yet he also competes for the support of the black urban constituency. Unlike Matanzima and most of the other Bantustan leaders, Buthelezi, despite his royal birth and proud heritage, is demonstrably a modern man and appeals to many young blacks, especially Zulus of course, who otherwise might turn to the South African Students Organisation or the Black Peoples Convention. Inkatha is an efficiently run and apparently well-funded organization, and Buthelezi himself is surrounded by bright young men who seem to know where they are going. He is also a well-known figure abroad and, unlike the black consciousness and the nationalist leaders, is able to move at will both inside and outside South Africa. His access is, in some ways, better than John Vorster's: on a trip to the United States in the spring of 1977, he had a long discussion with President Carter in the White House. To counter Buthelezi's mobility, the Black Peoples Convention has decided to launch a diplomatic offensive of its own abroad.

Whatever rocks lie in the path ahead, the achievements of the urban youth have already been considerable, especially the detrimental psychological effect their actions have had on the government and its external image and the beneficial psychological impact they have made on their own

parents and other blacks in the country. The older generation had given up
fighting the system and their childrens' courage and determination invoked
a bewildering range of emotions: awe, anxiety, anger, pride. Divisions that
were latent are now exposed. The middle-aged generation in the townships would probably be content with major social and economic changes
giving them a greater share of South Africa's rich cake. The youth, on the
contrary, want *political* change, and profound political change at that. Their
heroes are Samora Machel, Agostinho Neto, Fidel Castro, Franz Fanon,
Kwame Nkrumah, Eldridge Cleaver, and Malcolm X. Their parents' pan-
theon is milder: Albert Luthuli, Léopold Senghor, Martin Luther King. But
the older generation has also been politicized by the upheavals and by the
advance of black nationalism outside the Republic's borders. The rapid increase in the circulation of the *World,* the only black daily newspaper in
South Africa, and its sharp, often biting, editorial tone attest to the change
of mood.*

This group still has relatively modest aspirations, a fact acknowledged
by the Pan-Africanist Congress leader, Robert Sobukwe. He believes that
the bulk of the urban black population, though not the student radicals,
would be content with a package of concessions that included: equal pay
for equal work and the abolition of job reservation in all its forms, unfet-
tered rights to home ownership in the townships, and a promise of some
form of political power-sharing in the future. Sobukwe admits that if the
government made these concessions, it would not necessarily be in his party's interests, pledged as it is to majority rule. He told me he believes that
such a move would soak up much of the present discontent and divide the
blacks even more than they are now. But, apart from the issue of home
ownership, there is no sign that the government will offer such a package.
The white trade unions, under pressure from their members as the recession bites, are in no mood to allow Africans to climb higher up the job ladder, and the National party has turned a stony face toward any form of
power-sharing. The upshot is that the moderate urbanized Africans, who
feel no allegiance to tribe or homeland, yet are wary of the revolutionary
and socialist ideals of their children, find themselves moving into the terrain
of black consciousness and the banned but by no means defunct nationalist
movements, Nelson Mandela's African National Congress (ANC) and
Robert Sobukwe's Pan-Africanist Congress (PAC).

Support for the ANC and PAC within the country is difficult to judge. Both
were banned after the Sharpeville shootings in the early 1960s. Nelson
Mandela, almost sixty years old, has been serving a life sentence on Rob-

---

* The *World* increased its circulation from 131,000 to 159,000 copies per day in
the second half of 1976, a phenomenal growth of 21 percent.

ben Island since 1964 along with other leaders of the ANC. Sobukwe spent nine years in the same prison before his restriction to Kimberley in 1969. The rest of the leadership is exiled or in other jails. Mandela's wife, Winnie, has been in prison too and is now restricted to a small town 200 miles from Johannesburg. The ANC, as the older party—it was established as long ago as 1912—appealed to a wider cross-section of the community, and the PAC, a breakaway movement from the ANC in 1959, captured the attention of the younger blacks. But after both parties unsuccessfully launched violent revolutionary groups in the 1960s, support seems to have waned, more from despair than from disillusion with tactics or leadership. Africans who followed the nationalist flag in the 1950s are now middle-aged, and it is among this generation that the ANC-PAC allegiance may still be strong. In the wake of the student revolt, a number of organizations, like the Black Parents Association in Soweto, inspired by the older generation, have sprung up, initially to mediate between the students and the government but later forming part of a broad coalition with their children. The natural constituency for these people, politically involved and concerned yet not supporters of Gatsha Buthelezi, are the nationalist movements.

ANC pamphlets appeared during the disturbances, and there are believed to be ANC guerrillas training in camps in southern Mozambique. There have been a number of small border incidents with South African security forces in that region, and in April, 1976, the authorities announced they had uncovered an ANC recruiting network channeling young men through Swaziland to Mozambique. Since the riots, hundreds of young blacks have sought refuge in neighboring African countries, and a large proportion of these will probably join the nationalist organizations, repeating the pattern of youthful emigration from South-West Africa to the South-West African Peoples Organization and from Rhodesia to the Zimbabwe African National Union and Zimbabwe African Peoples Union. It is significant that the people now leaving are educated or semi-educated youths and already heavily politicized. Moreover, although they may not entirely agree with the doctrines and tactics of the nationalist movements, their experiences in the Republic convince them that there is no alternative to the armed struggle and that the ANC and PAC are the only organizations providing the means of employing it. It would seem, on present showing, that the ANC, as the older, established, and better organized group, has the greater support but that the PAC, with its more radical image, may close the gap as the struggle intensifies.

The relationship between the black consciousness movement and the nationalist organizations is important, perhaps critical, in the long term. Steven Biko pointed to the generation gap, which he thought is more marked at the leadership level than among the rank and file. Although agreeing with the basic aim of the nationalists—majority rule—the black consciousness activists have some reservations about the ANC's links to the South African Communist party and its Soviet backers and about the PAC's "racist" overtones displayed in its philosophy of Africanism, which states that Africa belongs by right to the black and the brown races but not to the whites. There is also disapproval of the feuding and personality clashes that have afflicted the nationalist movements in exile. Nevertheless, they agree that Nelson Mandela and Robert Sobukwe are the African leaders of the greatest stature in South Africa and the men whom they would most want to represent their cause.

Nevertheless, they also feel that the black consciousness movement has played, and will continue to play, a catalytic role in African politics and would themselves expect to have a voice in any future deliberations. The development of the Black Peoples Convention as a more orthodox nationalist party suggests that the young radicals sense there is a vacuum that must be filled. It is clear that they do not want Gatsha Buthelezi plugging the gap, but whether they see themselves taking the place of the banned nationalist movements, *faute de mieux,* is another matter. For its public stance, the Black Peoples Convention has declared its attitude toward the ANC and PAC to be one of "positive neutrality."

The potential of black power in South Africa eludes precise assessment; all one can do is identify the elements and stress the strength of the opposition. There is no doubt that a new mood of militancy and hope has been generated by the youth of the townships. There is equally no doubt that the black leadership is far from unified in tactics although the goal—black rule—is the same. The white government is marshaling its forces and searching for new ways to exacerbate black divisions. (The new constitutional deal for Coloureds and Indians is part of this strategy.) The traditional homeland leaders—Matanzima, Mangope—have opted out while Buthelezi remains resolutely in the game. The traditional nationalist leaders—Mandela, Sobukwe and their comrades—have been silenced but not eliminated by the government. The students have begun to build bridges: the coalition with township leaders of an older generation which has produced a new leadership for Soweto, the Committee of Ten reflects this trend. And they remain the central activating force in black politics in the Republic. They await the day when Africa, the Soviet Union and others can help their struggle through guerrilla incursions across South Africa's borders. Portuguese and Rhodesian parallels are misleading here; the South Africans have a more powerful military machine at their disposal but also have to cope with a more explosive black threat behind their backs. Internally, black power's stongest weapon, the labor force, is still the most difficult to use since it remains fettered by problems of organization, poverty, government repression and employer reprisals. When Aladdin's genie appears again over the troubled land it could be carrying a spanner in its hand. But it is much more likely to be a clenched fist or a gun.

CHAPTER III

Retreat into the *Laager*

In a moment of exasperation during one of his Middle Eastern peace-making shuttles, Henry Kissinger complained that Israel had no foreign policy, only domestic policy. The dictum applies with perhaps even greater force to the Republic of South Africa. It is the domestic policy of apartheid—that unique system of government which separates and controls the daily lives of twenty-six million South Africans on the basis of the color of their skin—that ultimately determines the shape of the Republic's relations with Africa and the world. Ever since the ruling National party came to power in 1948, the majority of its Afrikaner supporters have regarded apartheid as pivotal to their own survival, and the country's politico-military strategy has been largely governed by that premise. Successive South African administrations have stressed that, although apartheid can be—and is being—modified, it cannot be abandoned; it is an orthodoxy that has buckled a strait jacket around Pretoria's foreign-policy-makers. A senior member of South Africa's Strategic Planning Staff described to me the tyranny that this domestic imperative exercises over his nation's foreign policy. "South Africa's national security," he said, "is dependent upon its relationship with the international community, which is determined by its relationship with black Africa, which in turn is governed by its relationship with its own black population."

There are, however, three other important articles of faith that guide Pretoria's strategic planning: a normalization of relations with the black states of Africa, a loyal if increasingly wistful pro-Western stance based on mutuality of interests, and a significant strengthening of the country's economy and defense. To many analysts the strategy appears to be fatally flawed by its first tenet—the unswerving commitment to apartheid—which must inevitably, it is argued, render the second unattainable, the third unrewarding, and the fourth irrelevant. Pretoria's answer is that there is no alternative and that, given time, apartheid will both satisfy the aspirations of the majority of the blacks and ensure the survival of the whites. In short, South Africa's policy-makers have accepted the disability that apartheid has imposed upon them and seek to frame and adapt their strategy within

53

54 those limitations. There are a few small signs of heretical opinions developing within the governing elite, questioning the validity of the apartheid creed in the rapidly changing circumstances of southern Africa and hinting that a radical reformation might eventually be necessary. But they have not deflected the main thrust of South African strategy.

One of the ironies of South Africa, a country that has more than its fair share, is that, although apartheid is inextricably intertwined with the nation's external image, many of the men who shape the former seem to be remote from those responsible for the latter. This disparity did not matter too much in the palmier days when the Republic appeared unassailable and when foreign affairs could be kept at a convenient distance from the white voter. But as the battle lines have moved south, the possibility of friction and disagreement has been heightened, especially between those charged with executing policy—the diplomats, civil servants, and generals—and those who have to account for it, principally the politicians.

South Africa's external affairs are run by a small, tightly knit group of professional civil servants and advisers under the direction of the prime minister, with supporting roles by the departments of Foreign Affairs and Information. The two most influential men, for the last decade, have been John Vorster himself and his security adviser, General Hendrik van den Bergh, the head of the Bureau for State Security. The two men have been close friends since the Second World War, when they were interned together by General Jan Smuts for membership in a right-wing Afrikaner organization that opposed South Africa's entry into the war. Van den Bergh is one of the most powerful men in the Republic (the Bureau for State Security is the equivalent of the CIA and the FBI rolled into one) and plays a key role in the direction of South Africa's foreign policy.*

Vorster and Van den Bergh are the architects of policy; Pik Botha, the minister of foreign affairs, and Connie Mulder, the minister of information, the draftsmen. Each is ably aided by a senior civil servant, Brand Fourie in Foreign Affairs and Eschel Rhoodie in Information. The senior partners in this echelon are Botha and Fourie. Botha, who replaced Hilgard Muller as foreign minister in 1977, is an experienced diplomat and a successful ambassador to the United States and the United Nations; he sits squarely on the *verligte* side of Afrikaner politics. But confusion, overlap, and even open rivalry have, from time to time, characterized the relationship between Foreign Affairs, in its Olympian setting in Pretoria's rust red Union

---

* The Bureau for State Security (BOSS) was set up in May, 1969, by a special act of Parliament. Van den Bergh had been in charge of the Security Police before taking over BOSS. The nearest American parallel would be Henry Kissinger in his position as Nixon's national security adviser at the White House.

Buildings, and Information, in its more humdrum downtown offices at Ad Astra House. Technically, the Information Department fills the junior role in foreign diplomacy, but in Connie Mulder it has a powerful political figure, the National party's Transvaal leader and Vorster's heir apparent. At one remove, but not the less important because of that, is the Defence Ministry, headed by P.W. Botha, who is also deputy prime minister and party leader in the Cape Province. He is advised by the Defence Staff Council, led by the chief of the Defence Force, General Magnus Malan. On the fringes of South African diplomacy, yet sometimes crucial in its dealings with African states, are a few free-lance operators such as leading businessmen, academics, and journalists.

A striking fact about the architects, draftsmen, and builders of South African foreign policy is that their numbers are small and their tenure in office long. Vorster has been prime minister and Van den Bergh his security adviser since 1966; Hilgard Muller was foreign minister from 1964 until early 1977; Connie Mulder has held the information portfolio since August, 1968; P.W. Botha has been defense minister for eleven years; and Brand Fourie has held the top civil service post at Foreign Affairs for more than a decade. The formulation of policy is not such a one-man affair as it used to be in the days of Vorster's predecessor, Hendrick Verwoerd,* but it still remains a secretive, almost cabalistic business.

The South African government has no difficulty identifying its principal enemy as the forces of international communism. Yet historically it has been the black, not the Red, menace—the *swart gevaar* ("black threat") in the towns and countryside rather than the remote, almost mythical Russian commissar—that has preoccupied the authorities. However, in combating the first they have constantly blamed the second, seeing—or claiming to see—the hand of Moscow behind every act of opposition carried out by a black man. This view has made it hard for the government to come to terms with African nationalism, although much of its policy in dealing with independent African states and establishing national homelands for its own black population has implied a frank and unreserved recognition of the phenomenon. Officials still find it difficult to draw a clear distinction between African nationalism and international communism, perhaps because they feel threatened by them both. A not untypical example of that confusion came from Major General Neil Webster, head of South Africa's Citizen Force and a member of the Supreme Command, when he declared in a

---

* In his book *Notes on the Formation of South African Foreign Policy* (Pasadena, California: Grant Dahlstrom, Castle Press, 1965, limited edition), Edwin S. Munger listed the most important people making foreign policy as: 1) Verwoerd, 2) Verwoerd, and 3) Verwoerd.

speech before the South African Institute of Management in November, 1976, "As long as Marxism succeeds in impersonating African liberation, nationalism and solidarity, and as long as it is seen as an expression of black aspirations, the Republic of South Africa will be obliged to look upon her neighbors as potentially inimical."

To outsiders the conspiratorial role that Pretoria has ascribed to international communism may seem overdrawn. But to South Africans it is real and frightening. The government's own propaganda may be partly to blame, but the fears have also been fueled by the unrelenting hostility of the Soviet Union and the People's Republic of China, the installation of Marxist-oriented regimes in Angola and Mozambique, and the new and active Cuban role in revolutionary African politics. There is a certain irony here. For years the South Africans have been blaming "Reds" under their beds whenever blacks voiced their discontent; the sudden shift toward Marxism by newly independent nations in southern Africa, largely the result of uncompromising resistance to legitimate black demands by the white governments in the region, is turning this attitude into a self-fulfilling prophesy.

Pretoria's analysis, supported by many in the West, is that Soviet imperialism is entering a dangerously aggressive stage and that the Western alliance should support the South African government as the most effective bulwark against communism. The Carter Administration, while not ignoring the Soviet Union's desire to extend its influence wherever it can in Africa, believes the threat is overrated and, more importantly, that it is the inequalities engrained in South Africa's apartheid society that offer Moscow the most effective means of implementing its policies. Vice-President Walter Mondale, at his meeting with Vorster in Vienna in May, 1977, said: "We believe that perpetuating an unjust system is the surest incentive to increase Soviet influence."

Some supporters of the South African government feel not enough has been done to examine the possibility of exploiting Sino-Soviet rivalry and that it was a mistake to forge closer links with Taiwan. But Pretoria regards the Soviet Union and the People's Republic as a twin-headed monster bent on South Africa's destruction. The Soviet Union is seen as the greater threat because of its physical capacity to support military operations at long range, dramatically proven in the Angolan war, and because of its long association with the banned African National Congress and the South African Communist party. South African military analysts note that the Chinese dislike a high profile and, while always favoring the guerrilla movements not supported by the Russians, are reluctant or unable to provide the kind of backing for their proteges that the Soviets provide for theirs. Peking's backing of the pro-Western opponents of the MPLA (Popular Movement for the Liberation of Angola) in Angola resulted in a major setback for the Chinese in southern Africa. But, on balance, the South African government appears to think that Sino-Soviet rivalry can only intensify the campaign against the Republic.

Since the Portuguese coup, Pretoria's planners have had to watch a series of strategic developments, each one more ominous than the last,

over which they have had little control. Stripped of its white-controlled buffer states (Angola, Mozambique, Rhodesia and South-West Africa) and
faced by a hostile black Africa, the Republic finds itself moving into a dangerously beleaguered position. Its Western friends are still friendly, but in a
fair-weather sense, and are showing no enthusiasm for becoming involved
in the physical defense of the country, whatever the consequences. To add
to the gloom, the Republic's black population is restive, and many young
blacks are leaving to join small but growing guerrilla forces beyond its frontiers. The economy is sagging, white emigration is increasing, foreign capital is drying up, and South Africa's traditional enemies in the United Nations, scenting the kill, are redoubling their efforts. The already hazy distinction between black nationalism and international communism is becoming
murkier; the relationship between hostile external forces and the internal
problem posed by apartheid is tightening; the time scale needed to implement apartheid is being eroded. It is a situation that depicts the increasingly
successful exploitation of the blacks by the Reds at the expense of the
whites.

The pressure began to mount in late 1973. The Arab oil embargo
against South Africa and the steep rise in the commodity's price that followed the Arab-Israeli war in October were the first danger signals. The
embargo itself was not successful because Iran continued to supply the Republic's needs, although the high cost of oil hurt the nation's economy. The
principle of economic sanctions, however, has always been anathema to
Pretoria, and the oil embargo demonstrated for the first time that the Third
World could wield a potentially devastating economic weapon for political
ends.

In April, 1974, the Portuguese government in Lisbon was overthrown
by a left-wing military coup. The decolonization of Portugal's African colonies followed, removing the buffer states of Mozambique and Angola and
exposing the white governments of Rhodesia and South Africa to the chill
winds of African revolutionary nationalism. It is difficult to exaggerate the
importance of the Portuguese collapse. In the saga of Africa, April, 1974,
may assume the fatefulness that France attaches to July, 1789, or Europe
to August, 1914, turning points in history that consigned the old order to
oblivion yet failed to reveal the substance of the new.

A series of setbacks intensified pressure on the Republic. There was
the trauma of the Angolan intervention, the escalating guerrilla wars on the
Rhodesian and South-West African borders, the world recession, the steep
slide in the price of gold in 1976, the election in the United States of a
Democratic president pledged to furthering black aims at home and abroad
(which may result eventually in turning American benevolent neutrality into calculated hostility), and, most important of all, a black upheaval of unprecedented proportions and unknown consequences within the country
itself.

What are South Africa's strategists planning to do about it? Since they
see themselves subjected on all fronts to pressure masterminded by the
communist powers, they talk of responding with a "total strategic policy"
embracing activity in all spheres: the military, political, economic, diplomat-

ic, psychological, cultural, ideological, even the semantic. The concept of an all-embracing strategy to combat communism may be relatively new and not too profound in that it lacks an ideological base, but two themes, each with a historical background and a certain continuity, are evident. First, there is the military dimension: support for the Republic's friends and a fearsome deterrent for its enemies in Africa and second, the diplomatic option of trying to make friends with individual African states.

The purpose is to gain time. Time, for the South African government, is a vital resource more precious than gold. Gaining time is necessary for the resolution of the Rhodesian and South-West African problems. Time is of the essence in the drive for economic self-sufficiency, for there is a strong belief among the men who rule South Africa that, given enough time, the Republic, while never becoming completely self-supporting, can achieve such a measure of impregnability that nothing short of an invasion by a major power or a worldwide nuclear holocaust will bring the citadel down.

Time, it is argued, will dampen the fires of internal revolt, since the country's anticipated economic growth will raise the standard of living of the blacks and provide them with a vested interest in the status quo. Forward-looking Afrikaners talk of a relatively short breathing space in which apartheid—or separate development, to give it its modern name—can assume a human face. Economists, military men, and planners regard the same period as necessary to toughen South Africa's economic fiber and strengthen its military muscle. There can be no finite goals for such a policy. But that does not diminish its significance as a conscious and central aim of the government in preparing the country for the day when it may be subjected to a siege from without—be it economic sanctions, arms embargoes, or physical attack—and revolution within.

South Africa's reaction to the threatening situation that has arisen since 1974 has manifested itself most strongly on the African continent. Is there really a South African strategy in Africa? Or is it an ad hoc affair, a series of tactical responses rather than long-term strategic planning? Before considering the answers to these questions, it will be useful to take a brief look at the background to South Africa's relations with the rest of Africa.

In the early 1960s, the South African government, under the powerful direction of Hendrik Verwoerd, was preoccupied with refining the ideology of apartheid at home and fending off a mounting wave of hostility abroad. Verwoerd's posture was essentially defensive, even isolationist. The Republic that he and so many of his followers had dreamed of for decades had become a reality in 1961: Afrikaner political power was entrenched, the shock of the Sharpeville shootings in 1960 and the subsequent financial panic had been absorbed, and the winds of change that had swept most of Africa to independence had left South Africa's strategic and trading links with the Western world unscathed. But toward the end of the Verwoerd era—he was assassinated in September, 1966—events began to demonstrate the inadequacy of an isolationist policy. In November, 1965, Ian Smith cut Rhodesia's links with Britain, proclaiming his unilateral declaration of independence, a fancy name for rebellion. The prospect of legitimate independence for Botswana, Lesotho, and Swaziland made it clear to Pretoria that the process of change in Africa—and dramatic resistance to it in the case of Rhodesia—was also moving inexorably southward, although with the Portuguese holding on in Mozambique and Angola the white *cordon sanitaire* remained intact.

John Vorster, who succeeded Verwoerd, considered that a cautious "outward-looking" policy of dialogue with the moderate black states of Africa might bring rewards. More of a pragmatist than his predecessor had been, Vorster felt there were other ways of dealing with black nationalism than turning one's back and trying to pretend it did not exist. A number of factors made the timing for this change in policy propitious. The Republic, enjoying an unprecedented economic boom, was stronger than it had ever been, and internal dissent had been crushed with a heavy hand. (Vorster's own, as it happened, since he had been minister of justice and the police under Verwoerd.) There was also a growing cohesiveness between the English and the Afrikaner communities which, while strengthening the government, did not dilute the Afrikaners' political power. And abroad, South Africa had won a technical victory on the controversial South-West African case in the International Court of Justice, which ruled that the two litigants, Liberia and Ethiopia, were not qualified to bring the action, thus effectively shelving the case. Finally, Africa was divided, disillusioned, and leaderless; the euphoria that had accompanied independence had long since been dissipated by the harsh realities of nation-building. The Chinese prime minister, Chou En-lai, visiting Tanzania in June, 1965, announced that Africa was "ripe for revolution." He may have been right, but part of the continent was also ripe for dialogue.

The central fact about the new policy was that South Africa was operating from a position of strength and on its own terms. Its strategy was cautious and had limited objectives. There were certain ground rules for the dialogue, the most important one being that, while the Republic's dialogue partners might criticize its racial policies, they were not to incite or encourage others to interfere with them. The image Pretoria tried to convey to Africa was one of multifaceted benevolence: noncolonial, noninterventionist, and good-neighborly. The Republic, South African diplomats emphasized, had no colonial cross to bear, such as Rhodesia or Portugal had, and it was content to remain within its internationally recognized borders; it had no designs on any part of Africa. Moreover, it was willing to share its technology and skills with the poorer nations of the continent.

A new degree of sophistication entered South African diplomacy. Feelers were put out to a number of African states, sometimes through Western governments or at the United Nations, on other occasions through secret emissaries. The French, deeply involved as the Republic's chief armorer, played a key intermediary role with some of the Francophone states while the groundwork for Vorster's secret trip to Liberia to talk to West African leaders in February, 1975, was done at the United Nations by his ambassador and the visiting Liberian foreign minister. Multinational corporations also took initiatives or were used in the exercise. Companies such as Anglo-American and Lonrho which span the great racial divide of Africa, offered their personnel, private airplanes, and money to help oil the sensitive machinery of black and white dialogue. For example, the first step towards establishing direct contact between South Africa and Zambia which led to the release of the Rhodesian nationalist leaders and the withdrawal of South African police from that country in 1975 was taken over an excellent dinner in the Savoy Hotel in London when the chairman of Lonrho, "Tiny" Rowlands, and his South African representative decided that things were not going well in southern Africa and that it might worth be trying to re-establish contacts between Pretoria and Lusaka. It is noteworthy that this initiative, which was given discreet South African government backing, predated the coup in Lisbon by several months.*

Lonrho was also not averse to hedging its bets in the escalating power struggle in the region. During the Angolan civil war, the UNITA (National Union for the Total Independence of Angola) leader, Jonas Savimbi, was ferried to and fro on a number of his secret trips to Zambia and South Africa in the Lonrho executive jet, and one of the company's Mercedes Benz cars was put at the disposal of Joshua Nkomo, the black Rhodesian leader, after he was released from jail.

By the time of the Portuguese coup in April, 1974, a muted dialogue had been established with a number of African countries. On the credit side, Pretoria could count a breakthrough with Malawi (the only African country to establish full diplomatic relations with the Republic); working relationships with Botswana, Lesotho, and Swaziland; and friendly contacts with a handful of more distant states, the most important being Ivory Coast and Senegal. The South Africans found they had struck a common chord with several African leaders—Hastings Kamuzu Banda of Malawi and Felix Houphouet-Boigny of Ivory Coast, for example—over their fear of communism. They also found their offers of financial aid and technical assistance welcomed among the poorer dialogue partners. The debit column showed the rejection of dialogue by the Organization of African Unity; the break with Zambia, Pretoria's prime target; the collapse of promising connections with Madagascar and Ghana as the result of sudden changes of government; and a right-wing backlash at home that contributed to the first major split in Afrikanerdom's ranks since 1948.

The strategy thus far had not been a wild success, but in Pretoria's view, it had at least marked a positive beginning to a new and necessary era of realism in dealing with Africa. Secure behind the white buffer and

---

* An earlier attempt by Pretoria to woo President Kaunda of Zambia had ended in failure in 1971 when Vorster, stung by the Zambian president's public criticisms, published a series of confidential letters between them.

waxing fat on an apparently never-ending period of economic growth, the South African government appeared to calculate that disillusioned and divided Africa would put self-interest first, accept the friendly hand offered, and shelve, if not jettison altogether, the dream of "liberating" southern Africa. That the African states by and large refused to cooperate is not surprising. For them Pretoria was offering nothing of real substance. The three continental issues that concerned them most—Rhodesia, South-West Africa, and racial justice inside the Republic itself—were not on the South African agenda. It is true that Vorster was worried about Rhodesia. Neither he nor his predecessor approved Smith's break with Britain, but as long as the Rhodesians showed they could both defend themselves and maintain a businesslike economy despite United Nations sanctions, the South African government had little interest in disturbing the status quo.

South Africa's dialogue with the southern bloc of African states which included "captive" black partners like Botswana, Lesotho, and Swaziland, was helped by economics. Apart from dominating the region with its huge industrial and trading base, the Republic used its wealth to consolidate its position. Malawi received generous loans, and South African money and technical skills were prominently employed in building two major dams in the Portuguese territories, the Cabora-Bassa in Mozambique and the Cunene in Angola. The trade-off between cooperation with black states that were prepared to put economics before politics and the Republic's more pressing security needs seemed a reasonable compromise at the time, but it seriously undermined the credibility of Pretoria's outward reach for dialogue and acceptance in Africa as a whole.

The Lusaka Manifesto, drawn up by fourteen East and central African nations in April, 1969, and subsequently endorsed by the Organization of African Unity and the United Nations, was Africa's collective response to Pretoria's dialogue policy. The manifesto, which is still the core of Africa's strategy toward the white south, strongly reflects the views of President Julius Nyerere of Tanzania and President Kenneth Kaunda of Zambia. It retains its importance because of those two leaders' standing in international councils and their continuing roles in formulating African strategy towards South Africa.

The manifesto begins, like the American Declaration of Independence, with a commitment to the principles of human equality, dignity, and self-determination. The signatories admit their own systems of government were not perfect: "It is on the basis of our commitment to human equality and human dignity, not on the basis of achieved perfection, that we take our stand of hostility towards the colonialism and racial discrimination which is being practiced in southern Africa." They accept that there can be transitional arrangements in the reordering of the unequal societies and that the whites in *all* the southern African countries—Mozambique, Angola, Rhodesia, South-West Africa, and South Africa—had a right to be there. The manifesto even calls them "Africans." "We are not talking racialism when we reject the colonialism and apartheid policies now operating in those areas." The African leaders then clarify their tactics. "We do not advocate violence .... we would prefer to negotiate rather than destroy, to talk rather than kill, ... but while peaceful progress is blocked ... we have no choice but to give to the peoples of those territories all the support of which we are capable in their struggle against their oppressors."

The manifesto goes on to discuss the different situations in the various southern African countries. In essence, Mozambique, Angola, Rhodesia, and South-West Africa are seen as colonial problems. The solution advocated in each case is the same: self-determination leading to independence under majority rule. Once again, the African leaders stress their preference for negotiations and a peaceful transition; the alternative, they make clear, would be increased support for the nationalist movements. South Africa is placed in a separate category. "The Union of South Africa is an independent sovereign state and a member of the United Nations .... On every legal basis its internal affairs are a matter exclusively for the people of South Africa. Yet the purpose of law is people and we assert that the actions of the South African Government are such that the rest of the world has a responsibility to take some action in defence of humanity." The African leaders underline the oppressive nature of apartheid and point out that it is unacceptable to them because of its racial basis. Privilege or oppression in South Africa depend on "the one thing which it is beyond the power of any man to change. It depends on a man's colour, his parentage, and his ancestors. If you are black you cannot escape this categorisation; nor can you escape it if you are white." The manifesto draws the conclusion: "The South African Government cannot be allowed both to reject the very concept of mankind's unity and to benefit by the strength given through friendly international relations. And certainly Africa cannot acquiesce in the maintenance of the present policies against people of African descent."

The South African government rejected the manifesto as a basis for dialogue with Africa. The foreign minister, Dr. Hilgard Muller, admitted in Parliament that the document had some encouraging aspects, such as "the modesty of these people in regard to their own achievements, or lack of achievements, and the fact that they deny they are opposed to the whites simply because they are whites." But he added at a news conference in New York that the African states had refused to accept South Africa's "repeated assurances that this commitment to human dignity [the central point in the Lusaka Manifesto] exists in South Africa."

Today, the Africans regard this rejection as a lost opportunity—by South Africa and the West. They point out that the manifesto was essentially a moderate document. It acknowledged the right of all the whites who had settled in southern Africa to stay there. It recognized South Africa as a sovereign and independent state. It proposed no changes of boundaries. In South Africa's case, it advocated boycott and isolation if negotiated change failed to materialize, not armed intervention or internal revolt. Above all, it urged negotiation and accepted that change could not come overnight. In effect, Africa was holding out the olive branch in one hand while reserving the right to pick up the gun with the other.

Pretoria turned its back on the manifesto for a number of reasons. Dr. Muller told me that the hostile comments about his country by African leaders at the time persuaded his government the manifesto did not represent a serious attempt by Africa to come to terms. President Kaunda's foreign-policy adviser, Mark Chona, added to this interpretation by commenting, "South Africa objected to the armed struggle option and thus read it as a document of confrontation, not negotiation." But it seems that internal politics also played a part. The year of the manifesto was also the year of heightened political in-fighting among the Afrikaners and the breakaway of the extreme right-wingers under Albert Hertzog. The government could not afford to be seen as too "soft" on black Africa. South African paramilitary police were operating along the Rhodesian-Zambian border against black South African guerrillas. Contact with black states, with all that it implied politically and socially, was still a delicate flower. And while the South Africans understood only too well that apartheid was the central issue in their relationship with Africa, they rejected any suggestion that it could be a subject for negotiation.

An important military consideration influenced Pretoria's pre-1974 diplomacy in Africa. South Africa, like Israel, calls its military machine its Defence Force. The implication is clear: the military exists to defend the borders of the fatherland and not as an instrument of aggression or conquest. Unfortunately, the reality is not as simple as that. In the case of Israel, it is the borders themselves that are at issue, while for South Africa, whose frontiers are internationally recognized, the temptation to preserve white buffer zones or to establish moderate black states in their place has blurred the image of a purely defensive posture. As long as Portuguese-controlled Angola and Mozambique and Rhodesia were not hard pressed, the South Africans regarded the Zambezi River as their outer defense perimeter. Pretoria's foreign-policy-makers had serious qualms about the political and military viability of their white neighbors, but the buffer zone held irresistable appeal for those in charge of the defense of the Republic.

Today, the South Africans play down their involvement in maintaining that friendly zone, but there is no reason to doubt that it was intimate, though discreet. The most obvious commitment was to Rhodesia, where 2,000 South African paramilitary policemen, equipped with helicopters from the South African air force operated for eight years along the Zambian border until they were withdrawn in March, 1975. The South African rationale for this involvement was revealing. The troops were there, Pretoria claimed, to fight black South African guerrillas who were infiltrating with the Rhodesian nationalists: in other words, "hot pursuit" at one remove. The Republic also provided or channeled most of Rhodesia's arms supplies, and there was an extensive military and intelligence liaison between the two countries.

Collaboration with the Portuguese was equally close. Military and security affairs of common interest were discussed at regular intervals, and where South Africa perceived it had a specific goal, direct action (with Portuguese approval) was taken. For example, South African forces were operating against the South-West African People's Organization guerrillas inside southern Angola long before the Portuguese withdrew. Raids against the Organization's camps in Zambia were also launched from the Caprivi Strip, and the South Africans trained Zambian dissidents in South-West Africa and sent them back into Zambia.* There were never any formal links with the Rhodesians or the Portuguese, but neither was there any serious attempt by Pretoria to distance itself from these governments as long as the political cost of being on the side of the buffer states was compensated by the security they provided.

It would be an exaggeration, however, to say that the South African military were entirely happy with the situation. They could smell the decay of the rotting Portuguese empire and observe the impact of the world's hostility toward Rhodesia. They had no wish to become deeply involved in foreign wars and believed their role was to stand fast on their own borders. They made sure their activities beyond those frontiers were low-keyed, and it is significant that policemen, not soldiers, were sent to help Smith's government combat the guerrillas who began to filter across the Zambian border in 1967. South African military thinkers were also aware that the country's own international isolation tied their hands. Destruction of the black Rhodesian guerrilla bases in Zambia was considered a desirable—and feasible—military objective, but the repercussions in the United Nations and among the Republic's dialogue partners would have made it counterproductive. Military aims had to be carefully balanced against political concessions. Nevertheless, until the collapse of the Portuguese, Pretoria was prepared to accept the opprobrium that a close military relationship with its white neighbors aroused for the sake of the security that those states provided.

However, the underlying reason for the South Africans not taking up the challenge presented by the Africans through the Lusaka Manifesto was that there were no considerations of realpolitik to persuade them that they needed to. In 1969, South Africa was secure, strong, and protected by a belt of white-ruled states with whom it had friendly relations and whom it was helping with economic and military assistance. True, there was con-

---

* The most notorious case was in 1971, when South Africa conducted a small but determined campaign to "destabilize" President Kenneth Kaunda. Some of the rebels were captured and revealed the South African connection to the Zambian authorities.

cern over the lack of a settlement in Rhodesia and over the decision by the Chinese to build the Tan-Zam railway. But dialogue, on South Africa's terms, had already made some progress, and Africa seemed in no condition to put the threats contained in the Lusaka Manifesto into practice. Significantly, Secretary of State Kissinger and President Nixon came to the same conclusion when they adopted as policy the second option in National Security Study Memorandum 39, positing that the whites in southern Africa were there to stay, that the only way for constructive change to come about was through them, and that there was no hope for the blacks to gain the political rights they sought through violence.

The overthrow of the Marcello Caetano government in Lisbon in April, 1974, shattered these assumptions and introduced a new era of instability into southern Africa. The smooth trajectories of Pretoria's political and military policies in Africa were rudely distorted as the government found itself confronted by new pressures and unexpected temptations. The result has been a policy which was at once confusing, oscillatory, and, above all, tactical. South Africans still talk of an all-embracing strategy, but beyond the simple concepts of gaining time and of survival itself, it is difficult to identify more than a series of disconnected, ad hoc reactions to events as they occur. But the coup in Lisbon did lead the South African government to launch a series of political and diplomatic initiatives outside its borders and a more subtle and hesitant exercise within.

The main problem was not where to draw the defensive line but how to adjust to the new governments that were beginning to take shape and how to ensure that friendly or compliant men would control them. Rhodesia had been a political liability to South Africa ever since Smith's declaration of independence; after the Portuguese coup, it became a military one. With a population of 6 million blacks and only 270,000 whites, Rhodesia faced the prospect of black states on all its borders except the relatively short frontier with South Africa itself. For the Republic's generals, whatever residual appeal the Zambezi River had possessed as a defensive perimeter vanished. In the long run, the country was indefensible; the only problem was how to extricate the 2,000 policemen. Botswana, which has a 1,000-mile common frontier with the Republic, began to worry Pretoria too, because the withdrawal of the Portuguese from Angola meant that this large, underpopulated and impoverished country was no longer quite so hemmed in by white states. President Seretse Khama might, it was argued, be tempted to take a more independent line or, alternatively, find himself under African pressures to do so. In South-West Africa, where the Republic had important human and material interests and total power, there was no difficulty in deciding to defend the 830-mile border with Angola. The unfinished Cunene dam, just inside the Angolan border, and the constant threat from the South-West African People's Organization guerrillas operating there focused Pretoria's attention closely on the decolonization process that was about to begin in Angola. That left Mozambique, where it was clear that Frelimo (the Mozambique liberation front), Marxist inclined and triumphant after more than a decade in the bush, would take power.

In the expectant months that followed the military coup in Lisbon on April 25, 1974, the South African version of dialogue, frail and ailing, sloughed its skin and emerged as a glorious new creature called détente. It was Vorster's artifact, although he had a little help from his friends. His fundamental aim was the maintenance of stability in the region, and his means of achieving it, the methodical and peaceful decolonization of Mozambique, Angola, and Rhodesia. The ideal, a strong white buffer, was no longer practical. The next best solution was a chain of moderate black governments, preferably brought to power by pacific and constitutional means. The aim was to try to create new Malawis or Botswanas whose leaders, it was hoped, through personal temperament and appreciation of the economic and military power of South Africa, would become correct, perhaps even friendly, neighbors. But this time, Vorster and Van den Bergh realized that they would have to give something in return, because the balance of power in southern Africa, while still strongly in their favor, had nevertheless shifted. The time for dallying in the poor houses and debating societies of Africa was past. Zambia, also worried by the threat of regional instability, was the key, and Vorster boldly reached out for it; but first he set the tone of détente diplomacy by his dealings with Mozambique.

It is one of the ironies of the new order in southern Africa that Pretoria managed to establish good relations with the country that seemed most calculated to threaten it: militant, Marxist Mozambique. For the first time in the region, a white government had surrendered power; for the first time, a black government was taking over after a bitter and protracted armed struggle; and for the first time, South Africa found itself sharing borders with a revolutionary African nationalist movement inspired by Marxist principles and dedicated to ending white rule in the remaining portions of the continent.

It seems likely that the South Africans were half expecting a Portuguese collapse. During 1973, South Africa's political and military assessments of its Portuguese neighbors had taken a gloomy turn. What took Pretoria by surprise was the suddenness of the coup and its setting in distant Lisbon. A Mozambican or Angolan unilateral declaration of independence by the white settlers had been thought more probable, but a coup by the Portuguese army, disillusioned and radicalized by the long colonial wars in Africa, was unexpected. Hiding their private qualms, Vorster and his advisers remained cool and quickly took steps to convert a threat into an opportunity.

The South African prime minister made it clear that he was prepared to live amicably with whatever government emerged in Mozambique. He backed his promise by refusing to help a short-lived *putsch* by whites and dissident blacks in early 1975; by sending technicians to help run Maputo

port and the railway; by adhering to the terms of the Mozambique Convention of 1928 under which at least 40 percent of the Transvaal's trade was
routed through Maputo; by reaffirming the Republic's commitment to the
Cabora-Bassa hydroelectric scheme; and, most of all, by continuing the
practice, laid down by the Mozambique Convention, of remitting in gold at
the old official price of $42.20 an ounce 60 percent of the salaries of the
Mozambican miners working in South Africa, thus enabling Samora Machel's government to sell the gold at a considerable profit at the much
higher world market price. In all this there was a degree of economic self-
interest—South Africa needed the miners at that time as much as Mozambique needed the gold—but there is equally no doubt that South Africa
could have, with little cost to itself, made life much more difficult for the
new Frelimo government if it had chosen to. Instead, Vorster played his
cards impeccably, thereby enhancing his reputation for rectitude and fair
dealing, if not altruism, in a number of African capitals.

The Mozambican government's priorities, dictated by necessity rather
than by choice, have ensured that the economic facts of life have so far
taken precedence over political predilections in the shaping of policy.
Machel's main objectives have been to consolidate Frelimo's power and re-
structure Mozambican society on "scientific socialism" and the "universal
principles of Marxism-Leninism."* The exodus of the Portuguese and the
backward condition of the bulk of the population have rendered that task
doubly difficult. The closure of the frontier with Rhodesia in April, 1976,
and the intensifying border war have made Machel more dependent than
ever on his powerful southern neighbor, a dependency that Pretoria has
continued to foster and exploit despite the widening ideological chasm that
separates the two countries.

Two examples may help to illustrate this peculiar relationship. South
African Railways and Harbours, a government-owned organization, has
cooperated fully with its Mozambican counterpart in maintaining the rail
link between the Transvaal and Maputo. This cooperation has involved the
loan of locomotives, the installation of a new signaling system, and help
with the construction of a loop-line to increase the capacity of the railway
between Komatipoort and Maputo. The general manager of South African
Railways and Harbours has also energetically tried to persuade traders to
use the route and keep Maputo in business; he has received full support
from his Mozambican counterpart, a regular visitor to South Africa. Economic factors, however, have undermined Pretoria's political strategy: slow
ship turnaround times, deteriorating services, a general feeling of insecuri-
ty, and new bulk facilities in Durban and Richards Bay have turned South
African businessmen away from Maputo.

Pretoria has also revealed its interest in retaining strong links with
Machel through the Mozambican gold miners and the precious foreign exchange they earn for their government. The number of Mozambican min-

* Frelimo's third congress, held in February, 1977, adopted Marxism and the
"destruction of capitalism" as the official doctrine of the party and government.

ers in the Republic has dropped from the peak of more than 100,000 in 1974 to 48,000 three years later and is estimated to be decreasing by 3,000 to 4,000 a week. However this reduction has been less the result of a deliberate cutback by the Mozambican government than the effect of a change in the system of payment to the miners under which the burden of the gold premuim was shifted from the industry as a whole to the individual mines, thus making Mozambican labor much more costly than other sources of foreign labor. The number of miners may stabilize or even increase when the clause in the agreement that allows the 60 percent portion of their wages to be paid in gold to the Mozambican government at the official rate is deleted. This change will mean their labor will cost the same as that of any other migrant group. The loss in earnings to the Mozambican government will be serious—over $100 million a year—but there are grounds for believing that the South Africans will make up the shortfall, or part of it, with some form of governmental aid.[1] The Republic remains Mozambique's largest source of foreign exchange (around $300 million in 1975 but nearer $200 million in 1976). Although South African tourism, once a source of considerable income to Mozambique, has dwindled to almost nothing, the Republic remains an important supplier of food, especially staples like maize and wheat. The gigantic Cabora-Bassa dam project on the Zambezi River, in which Pretoria is a major investor and which was designed to provide South Africa with up to 8 percent of its energy needs, has been beset by a number of difficulties but has started to supply electricity to the Republic.

There is a double irony in all this for those who think in stark ideological terms and for those who mistake rhetoric for substance. South Africa—not the Soviet Union, not Cuba, and certainly not China—is the mainstay of Mozambique's economy. And South Africa, through this buttress, is indirectly undermining with one hand the country it is directly sustaining with the other: its good friend Rhodesia. History bequeathed the opportunity, but there is nothing haphazard about the intimacy of the present relationship. If the South African government does replace the Mozambican gold premium with cash from its own coffers, its manipulative powers will be enhanced.

The Republic's gains in Mozambique are tactical but important. The Maputo route is still the shortest and cheapest for the Transvaal's exports and imports, especially for the chrome ore that is mined in the east of the province. Mozambican miners are highly regarded, and although much has been done to reduce the dependence on outside sources, foreigners still account for almost 50 percent of the labor force in the South African mines. The most significant consideration, however, is security. In his famous "Crossroads" speech, delivered in Nigel on November 5, 1974, Vorster professed satisfaction: "The question has been asked whether Mozambique could possibly be used as a launching pad for people wanting to sabotage South Africa. In this regard, I have asked for and received assurances from Mozambique."

However, the South African military, worried about the deteriorating situation in Rhodesia, does not believe that Mozambique can be depended on indefinitely. The generals originally shared the diplomats' view that it was right not to interfere with Mozambique's internal affairs in the early days of Frelimo's takeover, although it would have been easy enough to do so.* But the military perception is changing, influenced by the growing militancy of Machel's government, which has recognized the banned African National Congress; by the expanding Soviet and Cuban presence; and, not least, by geography.

The Mozambican border, 360 miles long, is one of the most critical of the Republic's frontiers because it is close to the industrial heartland of the Transvaal and because its southern portion abuts onto populous Zululand. As Chief Gatsha Buthelezi has pointed out, South African blacks can now shake hands over the fence with fellow Africans who have won their freedom through armed struggle. There are reports that the South African nationalist movement, the African National Congress, is establishing bases in that long tongue of territory which reaches down to the Zulu's homeland, and there have already been a few border incidents. South African defenses along the frontier, especially in the Kruger National Park, which stretches for some 200 miles along the eastern border, have been strengthened. Swaziland, which shares a 275-mile border with the Republic and a shorter one with Mozambique, may also prove a problem despite its conservative government and its relatively relaxed relationship with Pretoria. In April, 1976, the South African police announced that they had broken up an African National Congress network funneling young blacks out of the Republic via Swaziland for miltary training abroad.

The South African military, while not opposing the policy of quiet cooperation with Mozambique, feel that once the Rhodesian crisis is over it will be their turn. When senior officers talk of "low intensity" operations and "unconventional warfare," it is the Mozambican frontier that is uppermost in their minds. Their reaction should Mozambique break the de facto nonaggression pact, to which Vorster referred in his Crossroads speech, is likely to be more subtle than the Rhodesian army's Custer-style forays deep into enemy territory. The South Africans look to the Israelis, rather than to the U.S. Cavalry, for their models, and Maputo provides a tempting target for swift and punishing reprisal raids in which vital installations and individuals would be the most likely targets if southern Mozambique became an African "Fatahland." The Angolan experience, bitter though it was, did bring in its wake the opportunity of "destabilizing" the enemy by proxy. There is no equivalent to Jonas Savimbi's UNITA movement in Mozambique; but Machel's government is not totally unchallenged, and opposition could grow internally if his policies fail to satisfy the postindependence expectations of his followers. One exiled movement, called

---

* There has been a historic temptation for South Africa to "straighten" the line by lopping off southern Mozambique, but according to a leading military strategist whom the author interviewed in December, 1976, in Pretoria, the army had conditioned itself to a Portuguese collapse well before the event. In a war game in 1969, attended by thirty senior staff officers, only one advocated South African military intervention in the event of a black takeover in Mozambique.

ZUMO, which encompasses a mixed group of Portuguese and Mozambican dissidents, is believed to be active with the Rhodesian forces on the Mozambican frontier and has supporters in South Africa and Europe.

South African strategists have also become more wary since Mozambique signed a friendship treaty with the Soviet Union in March, 1977, which, among other things, stated that "in case of situations tending to threaten or disturb the peace" the two countries "will enter into immediate contact with the aim of co-ordinating their positions in the interest of eliminating the threat or re-establishing peace." The *Washington Post's* correspondent, reporting on April 4, 1977, from Maputo, concluded that the treaty "clearly leaves open the possibility of Soviet military assistance to Mozambique in the case of an attack from South Africa or Rhodesia."

The South Africa-Mozambique relationship breathed life into détente, and Pretoria's subsequent negotiations with Zambia over the thorny problem of Rhodesia sustained it for a brief period. It had long been an objective of South African foreign policy to reach a settlement in Rhodesia. The breakaway colony was an embarrassment because it focused international attention on the Republic's vital role in providing economic and military support for Smith's government, thus contravening the United Nations policy of sanctions against Rhodesia. The sudden change in the balance of power produced by the Portuguese withdrawal convinced Vorster and Van den Bergh that it was time to use their leverage on Rhodesia in an attempt to find a settlement that would be acceptable to the whites and blacks in the country and to the "front line" African states (Zambia, Tanzania, Mozambique, and Botswana). Zambia also had good reasons for wanting to end the crisis. The country was suffering from the effects of closing its border with Rhodesia eighteen months earlier and from a steep decline in world copper prices. Kaunda was also concerned about the growing guerrilla campaigns in Rhodesia and South-West Africa and his country's host role to many of the insurgents.

However, edging Smith toward majority rule, which was what the Africans wanted and what Vorster had believed for some time to be inevitable, was one thing; ensuring a stable and moderate black government to replace the white leadership was another. Both Vorster and Kaunda were aware of the difficulties here, Kaunda because he had walked the minefield of tribal and personality conflict many times before, and Vorster because he knew how Smith would play on the divisions among the black nationalists—something the South African prime minister was accustomed to doing himself at home—and how he would use these animosities to get himself off the hook of majority rule. And then there was the danger of his appealing over Vorster's head to the white South African electorate if Vorster exerted too much pressure, or not doing anything if he did not exert enough.

Critics have been hard on Vorster and Kaunda for the détente exercise, but there were real achievements. The 2,000 South African paramilitary policemen who had been operating with the Rhodesians in the Zambezi Valley were withdrawn; Rhodesian nationalist leaders were released from detention, where they had spent a decade, and allowed to leave the country; a cease-fire was called for and partially implemented; and political activity resumed inside the country, while Smith agreed to talk to the nationalist leadership. South Africa demonstrated that it was prepared at last to put pressure on its white ally, and Zambia showed that the Africans, as they had promised in the Lusaka Manifesto, were prepared to negotiate a peaceful solution to southern Africa's problems while putting aside the gun. The high point, literally as well as figuratively, was the meeting between Vorster and Kaunda in a sealed railway carriage (courtesy of South African Railways and Harbours) on the Victoria Falls bridge in September, 1975. The carriage was positioned precisely halfway between white and black Africa and was as symbolic as any dramatist could wish. (An equivalent although virtually unthinkable scenario in Middle Eastern terms would be the Egyptian president and the Israeli prime minister shaking hands at the Damascus Gate in Jerusalem.)

But Rhodesia defeated them, its political arteries hardened by years of abuse and mistrust. Smith felt there were still no compelling reasons to accept majority rule, a concept he had spent his entire political life resisting. And the Rhodesian nationalists, hopelessly divided, saw no reason to trust a man of that ilk, a feeling shared by many African states which had been critical of the détente maneuver all along. In their dealings with Zambia, the South Africans reveal something of their style of diplomacy and its limitations. Vorster's method is blunt and straightforward, at times almost brusque; he makes clear what he can offer and invariably fulfills his promises. He sent an emissary to Lusaka in March, 1971, threatening to expose the secret contacts he had had with Kaunda over the three preceding years if the Zambian president did not stop attacking South Africa in his public speeches. Kaunda ignored the threat and Vorster, against the advice of Van den Bergh and some of his advisers, published the entire correspondence. But Kaunda did not seem to hold it against him, for he expressed satisfaction with Vorster's behavior during the détente period. The two men, apparently, got on well together, and later, when détente was buried in the ashes of Angola, Kaunda publicly described Vorster as "an honest man."

Not everyone in Zambia, however, has been so charitable. A senior official in Lusaka, interviewed in May, 1976, commented that, while the South African prime minister's performance had been good, it fell short of perfection. The package deal over Rhodesia had been flawed, he said, by the failure of Smith's government to release all its political prisoners and by South Africa's decision (presumably at the request of Salisbury), to leave its helicopters and their crews behind when the police contingent was withdrawn. Zambian officials indicated to me that they also believed that South Africa could have twisted Smith's arm more than it did, a belief substantiated by Vorster's ultimatum to Smith during the Kissinger negotiations in September, 1976.

Zambia gave South Africa no marks at all on the South-West African problem. The front-line states were engaged in détente—they rejected the word but agreed to the process—because they construed it as a legitimate means of implementing the Lusaka Manifesto, which specified three areas of conflict that required negotiation and settlement: Rhodesia, South-West Africa, and apartheid in South Africa itself. Vorster saw it differently. Rhodesia was fair game, South Africa off limits, and South-West Africa a gray area somewhere in between. He recognized the international character of the territory and its "colonial" stature. But, in practice, he treated it more like a Bantustan than a problem he should discuss with the African states. He flatly rejected the United Nations and South-West African People's Organization demands for the handing over of the territory to the world body, the withdrawal of South African forces, the release of political prisoners, and the holding of elections under United Nations supervision and control. Vorster also has a peculiar and almost pathological hatred for the South-West African People's Organization, which, he asserts, was "conceived in communistic sin." But behind the defiance were solid realities. South Africa had a much greater political, military, and economic stake in South-West Africa than in Rhodesia, and rather than go along with the Africans' proposals—direct talks with the South-West African People's Organization—Vorster launched the Turnhalle constitutional talks in Windhoek in a search for an "internal solution" that would bring moderate blacks and browns into a new system of government and also be acceptable to the local white population, roughly 12 percent of the total, which retains strong political and other ties with their kith and kin in the Republic.

In crude terms, Rhodesia and South-West Africa are both expendable, although there are important differences between the two countries. South Africa keeps Rhodesia going but it has no ultimate control, and more important still, the geopolitical facts (Rhodesia is surrounded on all sides but one by African states, and the white population is outnumbered twenty-two to one) have convinced Vorster's government that it is not in its own best interests to become further involved in a stuggle that cannot be won.

South Africa is as keen as the West to see a moderate black government installed peaceably in Rhodesia, but Vorster has put himself out on a limb by publicly identifying his government with Smith's interpretation of the Kissinger deal as a neatly tied, take-it-or-leave-it package and not a framework for negotiation—the African and British view. Moreover, the prospect of another radical black state on the border, if the negotiations fail and Rhodesia goes the way of Angola and Mozambique, is no longer viewed in Pretoria with the equanimity it was in the palmy days of détente.

The option that détente offered—Zambia and South Africa working hand-in-hand charting Rhodesia's future—is closed. Three other possibilities remain. First, a negotiated settlement might still be achieved with the help of the United States, Britain, and the West; but, although it might help the whites through enhanced compensation, guarantees, and emigration opportunities, it seems unlikely at this late, embittered stage to produce the moderate, stable government of Pretoria's dreams. Second, the South Africans could withdraw their limited but crucial logistical support—weapons, ammunition, and fuel supplies—and watch from the gallery as the drama ends, almost certainly, in an "Angolan" climax, the victory of the radical black forces backed by the Soviets and Cubans. Third, talks could break down irrevocably, leaving Smith's government to fight on with South African support but gradually being driven into a corner as the country slides into chaos. A fourth alternative, direct South African military intervention, was excluded some time ago, except as a mercy operation to evacuate white refugees. After the collapse of the Geneva conference and the failure of the subsequent Anglo-American initiative, it looked as if Vorster had lost hope in the first option, would at all costs avoid the second, and would settle, albeit none too happily, for the third.

South African military cooperation with Rhodesia has remained close. In 1975, the South African police were withdrawn, but thirty-five helicopters and fifteen light spotter aircraft were left with their pilots and mechanics. Under an operation code-named Polo, South Africa has helped to build five new military airfields in Rhodesia, the largest of which has underground hangars and workshops and can cope with much more sophisticated aircraft than those currently in the Rhodesian air force. According to a British journalist based in Salisbury, Rhodesian pilots have been trained on South African Mirage jets in the Republic, and close police and intelligence links are maintained between the two countries.

While from a military viewpoint Pretoria appears to be ready to leap either way, in or out of Rhodesia, as the need arises, diplomatically the South Africans have their hands on powerful levers and use them when it suits their purposes. The most important are Rhodesia's road and railway lifelines to the Republic through Botswana and across the common border at Beit Bridge, Rhodesia's only points of access to the outside world since the closure of the Mozambique border in April, 1976. There is little doubt that the South African government squeezes this delicate windpipe when it feels Smith is acting contrary to its own interests. The Rhodesian prime minister's initial reluctance to accept Kissinger's proposals, especially the key provision of majority rule, brought a period of "congestion" on the South African railway system which delayed Rhodesia's vital exports.*

---

* "In mid-August [1976] an estimated R$60 million of Rhodesia's exports, that is more than 10% of the total, was held up." (Johannesburg *Financial Mail*, 31 December 1976.) "Last August [1976] approximately 1 million tons of Rhodesia's exports lay stranded on the South African Railways and Harbours network." (*Ibid.*, 21 January 1977.)

An even more revealing insight into Rhodesia's dependency on South Africa was given in the famous Sutton Price memorandum, which was leaked during the Geneva conference. The memorandum, notes for a speech delivered to a Rhodesian Front meeting by Ted Sutton Price, a junior Rhodesian minister, claimed that Vorster had exerted a range of pressures on Smith to get him to agree to the Kissinger plan. The memorandum referred to South Africa's paying 50 percent of Rhodesia's defense bill up to the previous June but then holding out on future support; it accused the South Africans of closing the common border during Kissinger's visit and reducing Rhodesia's fuel supplies to a mere twenty-days' consumption; it also stressed the congestion on the railways and the large amount of vital Rhodesian exports stuck in the pipeline. It concluded: "The reason for the Rhodesian Front's failure was because of pressure put on Rhodesia. Vorster is the bad guy."

However, since Smith's acceptance of the Kissinger agreement, the South Africans have been more sympathetic to the predicament of their Rhodesian neighbor. Pretoria still fears an international escalation of the conflict or a situation in which large-scale slaughter of whites, particularly Afrikaners, might force the government to take action as the result of domestic pressures. But there is, nevertheless, a change of mood, which expresses itself through close cooperation with Smith's government, and a revival of the old debate in military circles about the advisability of more or less physical commitment in Rhodesia.

South-West Africa, however, presents greater responsibilities and temptations, although it is noticeable that the military show less enthusiasm for them than Pretoria's administrators and politicians. South-West Africa is not an enviable country to defend. Its northern border with Angola is 830 miles long and is straddled by the Ovambo tribe, the South-West African People's Organization's principal source of support; during the rainy season, there is adequate vegetation to cover guerrilla infiltration; across the frontier, a hostile MPLA government with Cuban military support is in control. Farther east, the narrow Caprivi Strip is hemmed in by Zambia, Rhodesia, and Botswana. The common border with Botswana is even longer than the Angolan frontier but possesses natural defenses with the Kalahari Desert and a sparse, nomadic population. South-West Africa is not a popular posting for South African soldiers and policemen, and they would be much happier and more secure defending the relatively short border between the territory and their own country, a mere 450 miles of semidesert. But South-West Africa's mineral resources, human ties, and strategic deep-water port of Walvis Bay make it too valuable to abandon without a fight. While South Africa has privately discarded the Zambezi perimeter, it has drawn a firm line across the top of South-West Africa and said, in effect, this is where we make our stand. In the long run, the territory may also become expendable if the pressure becomes too great to sustain—the South African government is nothing if not flexible in its foreign policy—but for the moment, there is a strong determination to hold the revolutionary African tide along that long and difficult northern frontier. A senior South

African official confirmed to me in late 1976 that, while a black Marxist state may be inevitable on the Republic's northern border in Rhodesia, a similar development is neither inevitable nor acceptable on the western flank in South-West Africa.* This view may still hold good despite Vorster's concessions to the Western powers over the formation of an interim government and the holding of nationwide "non-ethnic" elections under UN supervision before the territory becomes independent.

South Africa's future policy toward Rhodesia and South-West Africa has been considerably influenced by its involvement in Angola, at once the most tempting challenge of the détente strategy and its most bitter disappointment. The Angolan experience seems to have altered Pretoria's confident attitude of being able to live and let live with black neighbors regardless of their political ideology. But, while the South Africans now appear to be more concerned about the nature of the black governments that settle in beside them, they are acutely aware that the technique they adopted in Angola to try to influence the outcome is likely to be counterproductive. This lesson has been especially taken to heart by the South African military, who felt that their hands were tied in Angola and that much of the bungling in that episode should be laid at their own politicians' door.

From Pretoria's point of view, there were sound military reasons for intervention in 1975. There were the refugees, many of them Portuguese, to succor; the Cunene Dam to protect; and South-West African People's Organization (SWAPO) bases to destroy. There was also the possibility of influencing the composition of the future black government in the territory—there had been no such opportunity in Mozambique—because a civil war had broken out between the three nationalist movements. The SWAPO threat, containable but persistent, gave the South African military an added incentive for intervention, since they hoped that the Angolan group they supported would repay the debt later by curbing SWAPO's activities.

The South African intervention in Angola has to be seen, I think, as two separate phases. First, there was the purely military stage confined to the immediate border area. Here the aim was clear: a limited incursion to

---

* This is not the view of top officials in the Bureau for State Security, who, according to an interview with Arnaud de Borchgrave in *Newsweek* (25 October 1976), favor a conciliatory attitude toward the South-West African People's Organization on the basis that the organization will eventually take over anyway. There are reasons to suspect that the opinions expressed in this interview may have been a kite-flying exercise for Kissinger, then deeply involved in his new African diplomacy. But, genuine or not, this attitude toward South-West Africa is a minority one in government circles in Pretoria.

protect the Cunene Dam (in which the Republic had invested almost $200 million), help the refugees, and strike at SWAPO camps. The door was already open, the Portuguese having allowed their authority to slip away as the country dissolved into civil war. South African troops were operating freely in the vast open tracts of land on the Angolan side of the border by mid-July, 1975.[2]

The second stage was both political and military and was much.more complex. It was also, ironically, determined by the détente strategy. If there had been no détente, it is safe to say there would have been no South African penetration of Angola beyond the border zone. The basic reasons Pretoria risked a much deeper incursion were that Vorster was asked to do so by Jonas Savimbi, the leader of UNITA, which traditionally drew its support from the southern part of Angola, and that Savimbi's request received the backing of at least four key African presidents: Mobuto Sese Seko of Zaire, Kaunda of Zambia, Houphouët-Boigny of Ivory Coast, and Senghor of Senegal. The Africans' aims were substantially the same as South Africa's, that is, the establishment of an Angolan government of national unity in which the moderate pro-Western movements, UNITA and FNLA (National Front for the Liberation of Angola), would neutralize the influence of the Soviet- and Cuban-supported MPLA. This identity of interest and the chance to show the Africans that the Republic was willing to spend blood and treasure in a common African cause proved irresistible to Vorster's government. Pretoria was aware of the risks of such an operation, but the prize was seen to be golden. "If Savimbi had won," a senior official told me in Pretoria in November, 1976, "South Africa would now be a member of the Organization of African Unity."

The South Africans also probably considered that there was a "fail-safe" device implanted in the policy because they would be backing the same side as the West and that for this service they would receive due recognition and possibly material assistance. There appeared to be a belief, too, that South African troops, fighting on their own continent, would be regarded as generally more acceptable in the Western democracies than were interlopers like the Cubans, who had come from another hemisphere. In both these perceptions they were disastrously wrong.

At the time, however, a few weeks before Angola's independence, intervention on a limited scale was too tempting a prospect to pass by. Nevertheless, Vorster imposed severe restrictions on the size and scope of the adventure. The force involved was small, around 2,000 men; only armored cars and artillery were to be used—no tanks, infantry, or combat aircraft; the invaders were to remain as invisible as possible, posing as mercenaries and protected by a wall of official silence at home. The aim of the operation was to provide training and support for the UNITA and FNLA forces, to help re-establish them securely in their traditional spheres of influence, and to pull out by Angola's independence day, November 11. Pretoria was reluctant to make any long-term commitment to Jonas Savimbi and Holden Roberto (the leader of the FNLA), aware perhaps of the possi-

bility of stalemate and the suction effect, with the Cubans on the other side,
that a "Vietnamization" of the conflict could have.

Things began well. With South African help, UNITA strengthened its
position in the center of the country while the FNLA advanced toward Luanda from the north. The coastal towns tumbled one after another to a
mixed column of South Africans, dissident FNLA men (under the former
soccer star Daniel Chipenda), Portuguese, and Bushmen. This column,
code-named Operation Zulu, was under the command of an Afrikaner col-
onel who earned the nickname "Rommel" from his men as they swept
northward.[3] At this point, on the eve of independence, an element of confusion and division intruded into South African strategy. The Cuban and
Russian build-up had begun on a massive scale. The problem of the moment was not whether to buttress UNITA and the FNLA in their own
areas—that had been achieved—but whether to assist them to sweep on
and seize Luanda. There was, apparently, an operational blueprint for a
combined seaborne and land-based pincer movement to take the capital,
called the Bierman plan after the then chief of the South African Defence
Force, Admiral Hugo Bierman. A hawkish section of the cabinet, led by
P.W. Botha, the minister of defense, advocated the dispatch of more
troops. Some of the army commanders, especially those inside Angola,
shared this view. Others took the attitude that the job was already done
and that it was time to withdraw. Vorster himself was against sending more
men and equipment for fear that such a move would give the impression
that South Africa intended to conquer the country, an impression he
wanted to avoid at all costs. Savimbi and Roberto disagreed on tactics. The
UNITA leader favored restraint on the grounds that he felt he would not
be able to hold Luanda without overt South African support, whereas
Roberto, poised a mere nineteen miles from the city, wanted to advance
even though his forces were ill-trained and a large body of Cuban and
MPLA troops blocked his path. The Organization of African Unity meeting
on Angola was due in early December, and Savimbi flew to Pretoria to ask
the South Africans to hold on until the meeting was over. Pretoria told its
forces to wait where they were; and while they waited, Cuban reinforce-
ments and Soviet arms continued to pour in. A cardinal principle of military strategy—the clear definition and pursuit of the desired aim—had been
violated, and South Africa was to pay for that violation.[4]

Thereafter, the South African government was forced back on the
defensive, both politically and militarily. The initiative was taken out of its
hands, first by the failure of the FNLA to succeed in its bid to capture Luanda, then by the size of the Cuban and Soviet commitment to the newly installed MPLA government, and finally by the abrupt cutoff of American
support for its FNLA and UNITA allies by a skeptical United States Congress. It rapidly became clear that there were only two alternatives left:
South Africa would either have to send much larger forces into Angola or
pull out altogether. Pretoria began to receive signals that all was not well in
the United States even before Congress cut clandestine aid with the Tun-

ney amendment a week before Christmas. In November, the South African ambassador in Washington, Pik Botha, was warned by a group of conservative Republican and Democratic senators that the United States would not match the Soviet effort in Angola. Botha flew back to South Africa convinced that his country had to withdraw from Angola immediately.

In Pretoria, the decision was taken at the end of December and a date set in the first week of January. However, according to South African officials and journalists involved in the crisis, the South Africans agreed to delay their withdrawal after requests from Savimbi, at least two of the moderate African states, and the U.S. government itself had been made asking them to stay in the country until the Organization of African Unity completed its crucial meeting on the crisis later that month. The South African government felt partially vindicated in complying after the Organization of African Unity split evenly down the middle on the issue and refrained from condemning its intervention. By the end of January, the South African forces had withdrawn to the south, and two months later, they handed over the Cunene Dam to the victorious MPLA and pulled back across the South-West African border. Many critics of the intervention predicted it would prove to be South Africa's Vietnam; instead, it had turned out to be its Suez.

The post-mortem is not over, but the Angolan affair shook the rivets out of détente and ended the attempt by the white and black states of southern Africa to cooperate in establishing a new order in the wake of Portugal's retreat from the continent. The Angolan war resulted in a new and deep commitment in Africa by the Cubans and Russians and that commitment, in turn, brought the involvement of the U.S. government. There is no doubt that many black states shared South Africa's and Rhodesia's apprehension about the Angolan crisis. It was Kaunda, not Vorster or Smith, who referred to the Soviet Union and Cuba as a "plundering tiger and its deadly cubs coming in through the back door." Each side drew its own conclusions, especially in the context of the unsolved problem of Rhodesia. The Africans decided that, while Soviet and Cuban aid for the guerrilla movements was necessary and acceptable, non-African military intervention was neither. They were also determined to try to heal the divisions among the African nationalist organizations before they resulted in the kind of disastrous schisms that had rent Angola. They still welcomed the principle of negotiation but felt increasingly that Africans in the unliberated white south would only gain their freedom and stature through armed struggle. They also concluded that front-line solidarity, which had broken down over Angola (Mozambique and Tanzania backed the MPLA, while Zambia and Botswana supported UNITA-FNLA), had to be maintained at all costs. Finally, they agreed with the general consensus that the Soviets and Cubans

had won a singular victory, that the West and China had suffered a defeat;
that Africa had not reason to be proud; that blacks still under white rule had
received a significant injection of hope and their masters a corresponding
dose of despair; and that the time-scale for peaceful evolutionary change in
southern Africa had been dramatically foreshortened.

The South African assessment was bitter. Neither the iron fist nor the
velvet glove had been of avail: the military felt they had to bear the stigma
of defeat in a war they had not been properly allowed to fight, and the
government considered it had been betrayed by its Western and African allies. Many military critics thought that the low-keyed nature of the operation had been a major failing, that an all-or-nothing approach should have
been adopted from the outset. "We shouldn't have gone in and we
shouldn't have come out," one South African official commented wryly
after it was all over, echoing the opinion of several British and French generals on the Suez fiasco twenty years earlier. Certain sections of the army
resented the clandestine approach to the intervention and the way the
government tried to cover it up at home and abroad. This will undoubtedly
influence their attitude toward future operations beyond South Africa's
borders. Similarly, the limitations on weaponry and personnel irked the
military, although they understood Savimbi's sensitivity about overt South
African support. By all accounts, the army performed well on the battlefield, but there was some confusion at the command and logistical level, a
reflection perhaps that South Africa had not fought a war since 1945.[5]

The most damaging effects of the abortive intervention were not physical but diplomatic and psychological. A number of African states, of which
Nigeria was the most important, threw their weight behind the MPLA largely because South Africa appeared on the other side. Despite the Organization of African Unity's failure to condemn the Republic's role in Angola—
Cuba's intervention was not condemned either—South Africa remained
the pariah of the continent. It also became clear that the West had no desire to be seen alongside the South Africans in such a situation, although
Pretoria claimed, and evidently genuinely believed, that it was crusading
against international communism on the "free world's" behalf. South Africa appears to have misjudged the ambivalence of Western policy in Africa
and, more particularly, the mood of the American public in the wake of the
Vietnam trauma and the Watergate scandal. The Ford administration
found itself in a delicate position, on the brink of an election year and on
the wrong foot with black Africa with its Kissinger-inspired policy of deliberate neglect. There was little contact with the South Africans at the diplomatic level—Kissinger saw Pik Botha once during the crisis—and the State
Department denied emphatically that it had had any warning of the South
African military intervention. Even at the intelligence level, where the Central Intelligence Agency and Bureau for State Security exchange information on a regular basis, there were the inhibiting factors of the United
States' long-standing arms embargo against the Republic and a congres-
sional probe into Central Intelligence Agency activities that was in progress
at the time. Central Intelligence operatives working with Savimbi and

Roberto in Africa certainly had contact with the South Africans and may have led the latter to believe that since they were fighting the same enemy, American support could be taken for granted. The arms embargo, punctured in the past under the Nixon-Kissinger policy of tilt toward the white governments of southern Africa, had a few more holes drilled in it by the delivery to South Africa of C-130 parts and other military spares, which sometimes may have resulted in the improvement of the equipment they were destined for. But there is no firm evidence of American collusion in the South African adventure, although, once the South Africans were in, the United States did, along with several African states, ask them to prolong their stay until the Organization of African Unity's thrice-delayed meeting on the crisis had been held. The South Africans, in return, expected a friendly American gesture but received none and were particularly incensed when the United States joined in a critical vote against them three months later in the United Nations Security Council.

Pretoria was less critical of the African reaction but was nevertheless annoyed that the governments they had helped had jumped onto the MPLA bandwagon with such alacrity. Moreover, there was no way of removing the label "aggressor" that many of the Republic's enemies had hung around its neck. The South Africans could not prove, even if they had wanted to, that it was the Africans themselves who had invited them in. There were no written agreements, and in any case, Pretoria took the longer view that public recriminations would irrevocably alienate their dialogue partners, with whom they still hoped to do business.

Before assessing the full impact of Angola on South Africa's military, it might be useful to establish what the intervention did *not* do. The South African army, despite superficial appearances to the contrary, was neither mauled nor defeated. In fact, it was not greatly involved in direct fighting, the most common form of combat being long-range artillery duels with the Cubans. The only pitched battle of any consequence occurred over a contested river-crossing in which Pretoria claimed—and the Cubans denied—a crushing South African victory. Casualties were small: thirty dead, one hundred wounded, and a handful of men taken prisoner. The army was not pushed out, even though it was outnumbered by the Cubans by at least five to one; it went of its own accord and at its own pace. Morale was not shattered, although the soldiers were young and unaccustomed to warfare. There were no mass desertions, no significant draft-dodging, and no ground swell of antiwar protest, though there were individual expressions of dissent. The call-up caused disruption in civilian life, and the final cost of the operation, estimated to be $133 million, added a heavy burden to the country's continually growing defense costs. There is no doubt that South Africa could have committed much larger forces to Angola if it had chosen to. Several infantry battalions and a large amount of armor were standing by in the newly expanded military base at Grootfontein in South-West Africa but were never used.[6] Finally, counterbalancing the critics, there was a strong surge of white patriotism inside the Republic for the "boys on the border."

From the military viewpoint, the worst aspect of the abortive intervention was the erosion of the the South African army's credibility. Pretoria's generals stress that credibility does not reside in the mind of the one who threatens to use his power but in the effect, deterrent or otherwise, that it has on the mind of his opponent. They admit that their forces' deterrent image in the eyes of the Africans, and perhaps of the Russians and Cubans as well, has been seriously harmed by the Angolan episode.* The generals feel that the deficit in their credibility can only be made good when an opportunity presents itself to show that the Republic's political will and military might are unimpaired. What form could this take? The South Africans invariably point to Israel's example. The list of possibilities includes swift and ruthless reprisals against acts of insurgency, punitive hot-pursuit tactics regardless of the political embarrassment they may cause, the "taking-out" of vital installations in a country that plays host to hostile guerrilla forces, and pre-emptive strikes in a threatening situation.

Such a restoration of credibility would have serious repercussions, which Pretoria will have to grapple with. The South African army, the military strategists say, cannot afford to lose any more credibility, but the counterinsurgency tactics they prescribe would inevitably result in the Republic's being branded an aggressor by the Organization of African Unity and the United Nations. Fierce retaliation might also invite Russian or Cuban intervention at the request of a hard-pressed black neighbor. The diplomats argue that South Africa must fall back on its legitimacy as a sovereign and independent nation and keep its army firmly within its own recognized frontiers. The military men reject this view as self-defeating if—and they have no illusions here—the Republic is eventually faced with a serious insurgency problem along some or all of its borders. If strong retaliatory measures are not adopted, the enemy will be emboldened, the morale of the army will sink, and the local population will lose its faith in the capacity of the government to protect it. A new factor has entered the equation since the Soweto disturbances: any sign of weakness on the part of the Republic's armed forces could reignite the dry tinder of black revolt, thus threatening the army to the rear. The success of Frelimo in Mozambique and the MPLA in Angola has persuaded urban blacks in South Africa that liberation is at last on its way; any military success, no matter how small, by their own compatriots will strengthen their conviction that it is at hand.

One counterinsurgency tactic open to Pretoria is the removal of border populations, creating depopulated free-fire zones, but the South African military admit this can only be a palliative, not a cure. Creating these zones is also an admission that the enemy has the power to disrupt normal life, and relocation was resisted for a long time both by the Rhodesians on the Mozambique border and by the South Africans themselves along the

---

* One general, however, pointed out to me in Pretoria shortly after the Angolan war that the Cuban army would have no illusions about the effectiveness of the South African military because, as he put it, "We gave them a good thrashing."

South-West African-Angolan frontier. In both cases, free-fire zones were finally cleared, but the guerrilla incursions have continued.

Reprisal raids are another potential weapon in the armory, and the South Africans have been watching the Rhodesian drama closely because there they see their own future predicament writ large. Initially, Vorster was angered by Rhodesia's raids into Mozambique, but he seems to have changed his tune since Smith's acceptance of the Kissinger settlement proposals, and there are indications that the South Africans are informed in advance of these forays and have a hand in supplying and financing them. The South African generals recognize the military necessity for the operations and approve. Indeed, they themselves have used similar tactics in southern Angola, though more discreetly and with the advantage of operating in an area that remains unstable, with a friendly dissident force—UNITA—willing to cooperate against a common enemy: the MPLA government and the SWAPO guerrillas. Since Zambia closed UNITA's offices in Lusaka and established diplomatic relations with the MPLA government, UNITA has become, according to sources in South Africa, more dependent on the Republic for military and financial assistance. Jorge Sangumba, the movement's foreign minister was reportedly seen in Pretoria in December, 1976.

When South African strategists look to the future, their eyes are irresistibly drawn to the most vulnerable part of the Republic, the Pretoria-Johannesburg-Rustenburg industrial complex in the Transvaal. And the neighbor that seems to bother them is Botswana, with its 1,000-mile common border. Not only is it the longest of South Africa's land frontiers but it is also the closest to the industrial, mining, and commercial hub of the country and adjacent to some of the best farmland in the Republic. The Republic's borders are not particularly favorable to guerrilla infiltration, except possibly the area covered by the Kruger National Park, which runs parallel to the eastern border with Mozambique. Rather, it is the fragility of Botswana itself that causes concern. Botswana is a vast country with a tiny and predominantly rural population; it has no army and therefore little ability to control guerrilla forces; it is currently stable, multiracial, and democratic;* and it has a respected and skillful leader, Sir Seretse Khama.

However, three things worry the South Africans. First, Khama, although only fifty-five years old, is in poor health and recently had a pacemaker placed in his heart; the identity of his successor is not yet clear. Second, while Botswana has consistently condemned South Africa's and Rhodesia's racial policies, it asked for—and received—a special dispensa-

---

* Botswana and the Gambia share the distinction of being the only multiparty states left in black Africa.

tion from its fellow front-line African states to be exempted from any active part in the Rhodesian struggle because of its almost total economic dependence on the two white states. But, as the conflict in Rhodesia has grown, Botswana has been gradually drawn in, with the guerrillas using it as a sanctuary, a rest zone, and, according to some reports, as a base. Third, the advent of black rule in South-West Africa and Rhodesia may enable Botswana to play a much more active role in African affairs, something even its present moderate government has hinted it would like to do when less dependent on its white neighbors. Practical measures to help achieve this goal are under way. An all-weather road to Zambia is under construction, and the Botswana government has declared its intention of taking over the running of the railway from the Rhodesians as soon as it is practicable. Pretoria's view of the Botswana border was expressed bluntly shortly after the South African army withdrew from Angola in March, 1976: "South Africa's greatest vulnerability is along her borders with Botswana which gives access to the industrial heartland of South Africa. In a war of attrition, she would be forced to give facilities to communist-led armies."[7]

The South Africa military's view of a future black-ruled Rhodesia is that the realities of economics and transportation which currently cool Mozambique's ideological ardor will prevail, but probably only in the short term. Rail, road, and trade links are strong, but the generals are aware that African leaders, radical like Machel or moderate like Kaunda, are capable of economic self-sacrifice in pursuit of a political cause. Both men proved this by closing their borders with Rhodesia even though it hurt them much more than it hurt Smith. Rhodesia under black rule, with fewer workers in South Africa, a better developed economy, more trained Africans, and alternative outlets to the sea, will be less dependent on the Republic than Mozambique. However, its border with South Africa is much shorter and could be more effectively protected.

The largest imponderable that hangs over South Africa's military planners is the specter of black revolt—heightened by the Soweto eruption in 1976—inside the citadel while it is under siege. For many years, the military have asked themselves three separate questions. Can we defeat a combined Organization of African Unity army? Can we cope with insurgency on our frontiers? Can we contain an internal rebellion? The answers have always been—and remain—confidently in the affirmative. A new question has arisen since Angola: Can we cope with the Cuban threat? Again the answer is emphatically positive. But times have changed and the questions can no longer be asked one at a time, in isolation of each other. For those who look ahead, the ultimate threat—a combination of hostile forces, inside and out—has to be squarely faced.

South Africa has been pushed back onto the defensive on all fronts. Nineteen seventy-four was the year of surprise, 1975 the year of euphoria, and 1976 the year of pressure. In his New Year's message of 1977, Vorster stressed in somber terms that the Republic was more isolated than ever before. However some South African officials maintain that all is not lost in their country's relations with Africa. Détente is not dead, merely sleeping.

(Less sanguine observers would say it is in a deep coma.) States such as Ivory Coast, Senegal, Liberia, and Zaire will only remain cool while the Rhodesian and South-West African problems are unsolved. They and other moderate countries will respect South Africa's sovereignty once it has shed its colonial appendages; they might then establish more formal links with the Republic providing there is some progress in removing the worst excesses of apartheid. Countries like Zambia, Botswana, and Mozambique, the officials say, will also be less hostile when Rhodesia and South-West Africa have black governments installed; in any case, they will remain economically and geographically beholden to South Africa for some time to come. In short, the underlying realities of the Republic's military strength, its economic power, and its technological largess will reassert themselves once this disturbing period of regional adjustment is over and will place Pretoria's relations back onto an even keel with Africa.

That is the optimistic view. Already, it no longer looks realistic, and the support it has enjoyed within official circles appears to be diminishing. Diplomatic relations with Malawi or landing rights for South African Airways in Abidjan may be gratifying in themselves, but they are not going to play much of a role in the fundamental struggle for survival. The success of Marxist movements in Mozambique and Angola, with Soviet and Cuban support, has made negotiated settlements in Rhodesia and South-West Africa less likely. Prolonged guerrilla wars with revolutionary governments coming to power in the end are more probable. South Africa's unchanging support for Smith's government in Rhodesia, and its deep involvement in South-West Africa inhibit a clean and tidy disengagement from regional problems. Meanwhile the African mood, inside and outside South Africa, is growing more militant as oppression and Balkanization continue. That mood is reflected in the Organization of African Unity and United Nations resolutions directed with increasing severity at South Africa's Western trading partners and arms suppliers. The Lusaka Manifesto remains Africa's charter on the white south, but it is beginning to show its age. The document's major internal contradiction—Africa's acceptance of Pretoria's sovereignty, yet its pledge to take action on behalf of the country's blacks—has grown to the point where many African states are now questioning that sovereignty and suggesting the South African government has lost its legitimacy because it practices "racial and domestic colonialism."

South Africa's regional preoccupations, however, have not entirely deflected its energies from dialogue with other parts of Africa. Contacts continue with a number of African states farther afield, notably with Ivory Coast, Gabon, and the Central African Empire. Vorster went on to Switzerland to meet President Houphouët-Boigny of the Ivory Coast after his talks with Vice-President Walter Mondale in May, 1977. The Malawi connection remains firm, the two countries sharing with Rhodesia an unenviable isolation in African affairs. President Banda once talked of "killing apartheid with kindness" and does not seem to have changed his mind, despite the cataclysmic events that have occurred around him. Closer to home, the Customs Union provides a useful umbrella for working relationships with Botswana, Lesotho, and Swaziland, and South African trade with the rest of the continent, although only about 5 percent of its total, is still significant. The old dream of a southern African common market with the Republic as its dynamo has taken a serious knock since the Portuguese withdrawal. But the process of decolonization has had an uneven effect on the pattern of economic dependency. Zambia, with the Chinese-built Tazara railway opening up a new route to the sea at Dar es Salaam, has become less reliant on the Republic, while Zaire, deprived of the Benguela railway through Angola, is more dependent on the white south for the export of its copper and for many of its consumer imports including oil. And then for those who believe in the power of economic realities, the South African-Mozambican web of interdependence is a new twist to an old thread.

While the South African government would like to rid itself of its regional burdens and retire to the security of its own borders, it has to take into account an important domestic restraint. The conservatism of the Afrikaner electorate has been a constant factor in the formation of South Africa's foreign policy. Traditionally, South African leaders have told their people little of what they were doing in foreign affairs—developments were usually presented as a *fait accompli*—but growing proximity of foreign issues has brought greater visibility and a corresponding growth of interest. Military operations in Rhodesia and South-West Africa or on the Republic's own borders cannot so easily be tucked out of sight as they used to be in the Zambezi Valley and the remote Caprivi Strip. Any move that is interpreted as selling the whites down the river in Rhodesia or South-West Africa is political dynamite for Vorster's government. There are roughly 30,000 Afrikaners in Rhodesia, many of them farmers in vulnerable border areas, and about the same number in South-West Africa. Ties between the English-speaking communities in the three countries are equally close. The only English minister in the South African cabinet is married to Ian Smith's sister-in-law. Vorster's *bête blanche*, the extreme right-wing Herstigte Nasionale party led by Albert Hertzog, has lines into Smith's cabinet and parliamentary caucus and uses the "sell out" theme with some effect in its struggle with the ruling National party. That party retains its ties with the white leadership in Windhoek, and the Broederbond, the Afrikaners' secret "band of brothers," has active cells in Rhodesia and South-West Africa. There are also crypto-political right-wing organizations, such as the Southern African Solidarity Conference (SASCON), the Friends of Rhodesia, and the Candour League, which are vocal and highly sensitive to any hint of "betrayal" of the white cause. In addition, a residual feeling exists among the white electorate in general that, if South Africa has to take a stand against the tide of black nationalism, the farther away it is done, the better.

The litany of lost settler countries in Africa—the Congo, Algeria, Kenya, Mozambique, and Angola—is recited, and a great deal of "us too" emotionalism generated. Rhodesia today, South Africa tomorrow, they say. The hardheaded Afrikaners who lead the party and government think differently but cannot ignore these sentiments altogether. While governments remain in control of events in southern Africa, the white chauvinists are unlikely to present a serious threat to their rulers, although their nuisance value will remain high. But if the day should come when events begin to slip out of the hands trying to guide them, the right wing may be able to exercise an influence out of all proportion to its numbers.

South African foreign-policy-planners cling to the idea of the "total strategy" in which the many sources of their country's power can be used to bolster national security and acquire more time for the development of its racial policies. But even the most optimistic are beginning to realize that the options are narrowing. Offers of friendship, aid, technology, favorable terms of trade, and so on are not going to buy the Republic peace in Africa. The concept of South Africa coming to terms with the world via Africa remains valid, but it is unlikely to happen even if the Republic were to make substantial concessions over Rhodesia and South-West Africa. The phenomenon of the front-line states—Tanzania, Zambia, Mozambique, Botswana, and, more recently, Angola—has driven a wedge across the continent and ensured that South Africa will have to satisfy these states' regional commitments, which are backed by the Organization of African Unity, before a deal can be struck. The problem for South Africa is that these commitments include a radical change in the policy of separate development and backing for the black South African guerrilla movements. This in itself is not new—the abandonment of apartheid was spelled out in the Lusaka Manifesto in 1969—but it is now more firmly intertwined with the Rhodesian and South-West African issues, and there is a new mood of militancy and urgency thrusting it forward.

The South African government is fully aware of the linkage between its racial policies and acceptance of Africa and the world at large. In the early days of the détente strategy, this was privately, but never publicly, admitted. Pik Botha's famous speech at the United Nations in 1974, promising a shift away from racial discrimination and the easing of "petty apartheid" in South Africa, amounted to a tacit admission that the process of normalizing the Republic's relations with Africa could not be achieved by concessions on Rhodesia and South-West Africa alone. But events were already outpacing concessions, and it is perhaps significant that the session in which South Africa proclaimed in front of the General Assembly of the United Nations that there was no moral justification for racial discrimination also witnessed its suspension from that organization. Détente proved to be a sickly creature, born out of its time. Mozambique suckled it, Zambia nurtured it, but there was no time for it to grow strong. Angola dealt it a mortal blow, and the Soweto upheaval delivered the coup de grace. South Africa, under growing pressure, may eventually be forced to face the unpalatable fact that apartheid is the nation's ultimate and most dangerous strategic vulnerability.

CHAPTER IV

Fortress South Africa

A salient feature of the South African government is its responsiveness to challenge. It reacted swiftly to the regional vacuum created by the collapse of the Portuguese; it is highly sensitive to divisions within its white constituency; and it has shown no lack of will—though many would argue a profound lack of wisdom—in confronting the threat of black power inside the country. Not all these reactions may prove well judged in the long run, nor are they all unqualified successes in the short. But the important thing is that a carefully tuned response-mechanism exists in Pretoria and is in frequent use. Nowhere is this more noticeable than in the country's search for self-sufficiency.

South Africa, like most nations, would ideally like to be able to arm and feed itself and rely on no one for its energy and capital requirements. The Afrikaner, in particular, prides himself on his pioneer past, when his forefathers opened up and lived off a primitive land. This folk memory is partly myth. The frontiersmen of the eighteenth century and the Boer republics of the nineteenth depended heavily on black labor for survival, as the modern republic does even more so today. Rapid economic development, especially the growth of industry, has bound black and white indissolubly together and locked South Africa into the world economic system. This trend has become greatly pronounced in the last fifteen years and has been a source of both gratification and concern to Pretoria: gratifying because the flourishing economy has strengthened the government at home while creating new links of mutual economic interest abroad; worrying because prosperity has done little to check the country's diplomatic isolation or to satisfy the political aspirations of its nonwhite population. Pretoria has few illusions about the future and is girding its loins for further isolation and perhaps, eventually, for some kind of siege. The methods adopted include a bid to make the West more aware of the value of the Republic's strategic geography and mineral resources, a massive *étatist* effort to bolster its defense and energy capacities, a two-pronged bid to achieve security by expanding its economic infrastructure at home and diversifying its trading 87 partners abroad, and a search for new allies among other internationally isolated nations.

The quest for self-sufficiency began in the early 1960s when economic sanctions were first seriously considered in the United Nations and when the United States and Britain imposed their arms embargoes. It continued during the boom years of that decade, prompted more at that time by the needs of a rapidly expanding economy than by threats from outside. But even then the government devoted much of its energies to making good the country's deficiencies, particularly oil. Defense spending rose rapidly, despite the fact that the fires of internal revolt had been doused and the white buffer zone to the north was still intact. The development of nuclear power was given high priority, and the Republic moved steadily toward the ability to produce an atomic bomb. The Arab oil boycott in October, 1973, confirmed Pretoria's fears, and, though ineffective, it gave a new impetus to the concept of self-sufficiency as part of the government's overall strategy to ward off the new pressures assailing it.

South Africa is neither an underdeveloped nor a developed nation but lies somewhere in between. This suggests a vulnerability, and the parameters of the Republic's dependence on the rest of the world, particularly on the West, can easily be defined. South Africa's greatest material needs are oil, arms, technology, and capital. On a psychological plane, it craves acceptance as a member of the Western community of civilized, capitalist, and Christian democracies. Even more fundamentally, however, the Republic seeks physical protection should all its efforts fail and the forces of darkness threaten to engulf it.

In return, Pretoria holds out a number of attractive inducements. The West and Japan look to South Africa for gold (75 percent of the noncommunist world's reserves), platinum (89 percent), chrome (80 percent), uranium (25 percent), manganese (60 percent), titanium (50 percent), vanadium (48 percent), and large reserves of coal. The Republic also offers a rewarding market, one of the best returns on investment anywhere in the world (averaging 15-17 percent, though often much higher in the mining sector),* and a stable and well-managed economy on a continent not remarkable for either.

It has been a constant theme of South Africa's search for a secure niche in the Western community to stress its strategic importance to the West. It offers as bait its commanding position over the Cape sea route, its excellent ports, and its small but effective military forces. However, the West has shown a growing reluctance to bite. The United States imposed

---

* Since 1975, the rate has dropped considerably because of economic recession and political uncertainty.

an arms embargo on the Republic in 1963 and has not allowed naval vessels to visit since 1967. Britain no longer sells arms to South Africa and ended the Simonstown naval agreement in 1974. Even France has finally announced its intention of banning South African arms sales. There have, admittedly, been periods of backsliding. Britain's Tory government reversed the arms embargo in 1971, but the Labour administration clamped it on again three years later. Some loopholes have appeared in the American boycott (the sale of helicopters and light aircraft, for example), and it is still unclear how effective the new French policy will be. The closure of the Suez Canal in 1967 and the growth of the Soviet fleet in the Indian Ocean appeared to strengthen South Africa's strategic importance to the West, and Pretoria's principal lobbyists there—naval men, conservative politicians, and arms manufacturers—made greater efforts to achieve some relaxation of the embargoes by stressing the vulnerability of the Cape life line. Since then the canal has reopened, the Soviet threat continues to provoke contradictory assessments, and a new government in Washington has begun to make a fresh analysis of Western interests in the region.

The inescapable reality is the conviction in the Western alliance that as long as the whites rule South Africa, the strategic inducements so generously offered are unlikely to be withheld in time of need or given to someone else. If, for example, the West suddenly needed the Simonstown naval facility and South African military cooperation to defend the Cape route, Pretoria would be only too happy to oblige. The air would no doubt be thick with "I told you so's," but nothing would please the South Africans more. Vorster cannot play the nonaligned game the way other African countries can.* South Africa is a captive of the West by the nature of its history and its system of government, and it has to take what crumbs of comfort fall or are surreptitiously pushed off the Western table.

There are many in the West who share Pretoria's view that South Africa is the key to their own interests in the region and that the Republic is the Soviet Union's prime target in Africa. Concern about communist encroachment is also shared, but there is a difference, growing wider, it would seem, as pressures mount, about how this threat can best be checked. The South African government stresses that the preservation of white rule as it stands is the most effective bulwark against the Red tide, while the West feels that a new order in which the Republic's nonwhite population is given a meaningful share of political and economic power is the most effective way to stem the tide and preserve South African and Western interests. Although continuing to express a desire for peaceful and evolutionary change, the South Africans are becoming increasingly skeptical about their capacity to satisfy their critics, given their own carefully defined terms of reference. Pretoria, in short, is looking for assistance in order to confront

---

* Two classic examples of a Western-created vacuum being filled by the East in Africa were Egypt's invitation to the Russians to build the Aswan Dam and Tanzania's decision to ask the Chinese to construct the Tazara railroad.

black power supported by the Soviet Union, while the West is searching for a way to defuse it.

The changing balance of power in southern Africa has produced a paradox in South Africa's relationship with the West. On the one hand, there has been a tactical closing of the gap, best illustrated by Kissinger's meetings with Vorster over Rhodesia and Britain's attempts to persuade South Africa to maintain pressure on Smith to keep Rhodesian negotiations alive. On the other, the West has begun to distance itself from the Republic as political uncertainties grow and as the potential conflict between its interests in black Africa and South Africa is reassessed. The mixture of strategic disengagement and tactical involvement became apparent during the Angolan civil war. Pretoria had preached interminably about the dangers of communism in Africa, but when the South African army sallied forth to confront the Cubans in Angola, it found itself on its own. The United States, while not publicly condoning South African military intervention, found that intervention useful as a means of forcing a stalemate, if only temporarily, while other methods of blocking Cuban power and Soviet influence were explored. The Soweto riots produced a hardening of Western attitudes toward Vorster's government that is likely to have long-term implications—a cooling of diplomatic relations and the drying-up of loans and new investment, for example—but that strategic retrenchment did not stop Kissinger from launching his tactical Rhodesian initiative involving, as it was bound to, close cooperation with Vorster's government.

The economic needs of the Western nations also play a part in sustaining their tactical links with South Africa. In the post-1973 world, the industrial countries are struggling to find new markets and ensure reliable supplies of energy and raw materials as they haul themselves out of the worst recession since the 1930s. South Africa's treasure trove is too tempting to be ignored. Britain, particularly, is in an invidious position. The ruling Labour party, despite its ideological hostility toward South Africa, has concluded that the country could not afford to tamper with its South African connection.* This assessment, coming from the political party that had imposed an arms embargo on South Africa and is a sworn enemy of apartheid, reflected the perilous state of the national economy and Britain's large economic stake in the Republic. Other European countries are not in such a captive position, but the eagerness to sell nuclear technology to South Africa has demonstrated that, despite all the obvious political drawbacks, the South African economy continues to have formidable drawing power. The United States and West Germany, under pressure from anti-South Africa lobbies, backed down, while France, in a characteristically single-minded way, concluded a $1-billion contract in 1976 to build a nuclear power plant in the Republic.

The day-to-day paramountcy of economic factors seems to have produced a change in the perceived value of those elements which link the

---

* South Africa accounts for 12 percent of the United Kingdom's exports. Britain is the largest foreign investor in the Republic, with more than $5 billion at stake.

West and South Africa, a trend that suggests their identity of interest will lie not so much in strategic geography or in anticommunist orthodoxy—Pretoria's two strongest suits in the 1960s—as in South Africa's desirability as a valuable market, a repository of large and fruitful investments, and a source of vital minerals. The reopening of the Suez Canal and the new importance attached to economic resources may have helped to change the relative value of these priorities in some people's minds. While South African spokesmen often lay greater stress on resources than on geography when arguing for closer ties with the West, Western military analysts tend to regard the crucial minerals (chrome, vanadium, titanium, and uranium in particular) and the Cape route as of equal importance, while Western opponents of South Africa dismiss them as of equal irrelevance.

There are a number of reasons behind the West's cautious realignment away from South Africa. The first is the growing political influence of the African states, particularly the front-line nations. Led by seasoned and respected leaders such as Julius Nyerere, Kenneth Kaunda, and Seretse Khama, they have become deeply and irreversibly involved in shaping the future of southern Africa. They acted as midwife at the birth of Mozambique and, although unable to do much about the Caesarean that brought forth Angola, are now at Rhodesia's bedside and have South-West Africa scheduled for the delivery table. The shifting balance of power in the region has greatly enhanced the roles of these front-line presidents, who have been joined by Agostinho Neto of Angola, not in the least because they control the territories from which the guerrilla assaults on Rhodesia and South-West Africa are launched. Kissinger's Rhodesian diplomacy relied heavily on the front-line leaders. Similarly, any negotiations that may take place in the future on the international status of South-West Africa will have to be conducted through these channels because the presidents stand firmly behind the South-West African People's Organization. The African presidents' role, provided they remain united and retain the confidence of the Organization of African Unity, has ominous implications for Pretoria. The momentum of African involvement in the decolonization of southern Africa will not be easy to halt. South Africa clearly sees the surgeon's knife moving closer as it protests vehemently that its own flesh is healthy and the tumor of black discontent, which it does its best to conceal, is subsiding.

A second reason for the West's caution is that, behind the front line, the rest of Africa is beginning to move. The Organization of African Unity has not been renowned for either its effectiveness or its unity.* African attempts to boycott South Africa, which date from the organization's founding in 1963, have not been successful, but they have helped to maintain an atmosphere of isolation and hostility around South Africa and to bring pressure to bear on those who help the Republic. Now a number of the Organization of African Unity's more powerful members are beginning to ap-

---

* One disillusioned member—the leader of a small country who shall be nameless—remarked after a particularly grueling and inconclusive summit meeting that the only true word in the Organization of African Unity's title was *of*.

ply the sanctions that have been at their fingertips for years but rarely used. Nigeria, a major oil supplier to the United States and Western Europe, is probably the best example and another place where political and economic considerations may interact in the formation of new pressures against South Africa.* Political power, as Chairman Mao observed, grows out of the barrel of a gun. That remains as true as it was in 1938, but today power can also be found in a vital resource. The leverage of the Organization of Petroleum Exporting Countries (OPEC) has not been lost on other Third World nations with important resources. The various meetings between producer and consumer countries have yet to result in a new world economic order, but the producers know that unity of purpose and collective bargaining are essential if their interests are to be safeguarded.

There are also signs that African diplomatic pressure is beginning to count at last. President Valéry Giscard d'Estaing of France certainly took that pressure into account when he reversed his country's arms policy, although it did not stop the conclusion of the nuclear package with South Africa in May, 1976. African lobbying in the United Nations resulted in the suspension of South Africa from the General Assembly in 1974 and in the deadline for elections in South-West Africa set by the Security Council in January, 1976, for August of the same year, which undoubtedly helped to exert pressure on the South African-sponsored Turnhalle constitutional conference to produce a date for independence of the territory. While it is fashionable to dismiss the debates and resolutions of the world body, there is no doubt that the Western powers (especially the United States, Britain, and France, South Africa's traditional supporters in the Security Council) do their best to avoid using their vetoes in defense of the Republic.

A third development of immense importance in the changing nature of the West's relations with South Africa is the phenomenon of black consciousness or, perhaps more accurately, of racial consciousness throughout the world. The polarization of racial and ethnic divisions, seemingly more pronounced and less responsive to rational solutions than ever before, has greatly sensitized Western democracies to the issue of race. To people already caught up in racial, ethnic, or religious confrontations—South Africans, Rhodesians, Kurds, Lebanese, Cypriots, to name but a few—the bitterness and irreconcilability of the problem tend to preclude all but violent or separatist solutions. However, to democratic governments, such as Britain and the United States, which have potential or actual racial confrontations on their hands that could escalate further, the warning has been salutary. The profile of the problem and the dangers it presents have been

---

* Nigeria's commissioner for external affairs, Brigidier Joseph Garba, said at a debate on South Africa in the United Nations Security Council in March, 1977, that the time had come to consider seriously what to do about foreign investors in black Africa who have a major stake in the South African economy. (Colin Legum, *Observer* [London], 27 March 1977.) In 1975 Nigeria supplied 12 percent of the United States' imported oil; a year later the proportion had risen to 14 percent, making Nigeria the second largest oil exporter, after Saudi Arabia, to the United States. (Petroleum Industry Research Foundation, Inc., New York, March 1977.)

heightened by the politicization of blacks in Western countries, especially in the United States. American black elites, having passed through an emotional, romanticized, and often less than well-informed phase of identifying with Mother Africa in the 1960s, are now, in a much more realistic way, settling down to the task of trying to influence their government's policies in that continent. The painful and spectacular growth of black consciousness within South Africa, coinciding with expanding racial wars in Rhodesia and South-West Africa, has only served to accelerate this process.

The fundamental problem for South Africa in its dealings with the West is the racial shadow that never leaves its side. The stigma of its apartheid policies rules out overt alliances with Western powers, although some covert liaison and much sympathy remain. The South Africans are realisitic enough to know that the West does not want to be seen to be helping them too much. But they claim they are not making excessive demands, just a little understanding, a little time, and business as usual. The government is sparing no effort to get its point across, especially in the United States, where millions of dollars is being spent on publicity and lobbying. One Madison Avenue public relations firm, Sidney S. Baron, Inc. (which also handles Taiwan's interest), is receiving $1,000 a day for its handling of the South African account. Pretoria is particularly concerned that the Western powers, notably the United States, Britain, and France, will continue to shield it at the United Nations by exercising their Security Council vetoes.

There seems to be a psychological failure on the part of South African officials to understand how much society and standards have changed in the lands of their ancestors. Strains of puritanism and persecution recur often in the government's rhetoric. P.W. Botha, minister of defense and Vorster's deputy prime minister, wrote in 1973:

> Like the rest of the Free World, the Republic of South Africa is
> a target for international communism and its cohorts—leftist ac-
> tivists, exaggerated humanism, permissiveness, materialism and
> related ideologies. In addition, the Republic has been singled
> out as a special target for the by-products of their ideologies,
> such as black racialism, exaggerated individual freedom, one-
> man-one-vote, and a host of other slogans employed against us
> on a basis of double standards.[1]

Vorster himself, in his New Year's eve speech at the beginning of 1977, castigated the West as "a weak-willed highly technocratic free world in which freedom borders on licence."

Within this broad area of misconception, the South Africans' greatest myopia is over race. This is not surprising, since most white South Africans identify racial separation and supremacy with their own survival. Virtually everything the Nationalists have done since 1948 has sustained this belief, and South Africans are now in danger of being hoist with their own petard as they depict their policies as based not on race at all but on ethnic square-dealing. Western governments feel they can show some sympathy with ethnicity, since many of their citizens cherish their ethnic origins—although there are limits, too—but race in the last quarter of the twentieth century is a much more delicate subject. Countries that practice racial discrimination present themselves as clear targets to the Western democracies, which profess to be guided by humanitarian and liberal ideals, and to the Third World countries, which have only recently emerged from an era of discrimination themselves. To the West and to the Third World, South Africa still appears a blatantly racially discriminatory society in spite of its new ethnic apparel.

The Portuguese withdrawal from Africa left large gaps in the white buffer zone that had formerly insulated South Africa from the black states. The Angolan war demonstrated the new reluctance on the part of the West, especially the United States, to become involved in a Third World conflict, even though it was clear this decision would lead to a significant increase of Soviet prestige and influence on the African continent. The decolonization of Rhodesia and South-West Africa will leave South Africa facing independent black states on all its borders. In the breast of most white South Africans beats a hope that, in the last resort, the West will come to their side. However, no white government and certainly no Afrikaner government can plan its strategy on that wishful premise. The days of the cold war are over; Europe has lost its will and power to fight foreign wars; no American voter wants another Vietnam;* and conflicts on and about race are not the sort of thing the West wants to become embroiled in even if important strategic, economic, and kinship considerations are at stake. The arrival of a Democratic administration under Jimmy Carter in Washington and its tilt toward black governments in Africa reinforces this trend of nonintervention. The Western connection is fading. The South African fortress is increasingly beleaguered and its white defenders, as well as its black opponents, know it.

"Defence is of much more importance than opulence," Adam Smith wrote in the late eighteenth century. The South Africans have taken his dictum seriously, although over the last decade or so Pretoria has managed to have its cake and eat it, to strengthen the country's security without imperiling its affluence. That situation may change as the government spends more on its armed forces and squeezes the economy in preparation for the siege it clearly expects in the future. It is no secret that defense has the top priority and that expenditure has climbed dramatically as the instability of southern Africa has increased. In 1975, $860 million was spent on the

* A factor in any U.S. military intervention in Africa, which was not a serious consideration in Vietnam, is the racial composition of the U.S. Army, 22 percent of which is black.

armed forces; in 1976, the figure had almost doubled, to $1.6 billion; and in
1977, it had increased to $1.9 billion. In the last five years, the defense burden has quadrupled, and by the 1977-78 budget, it was accounting for a fifth of total expenditure. However, although high and an increasing strain on the government's resources, this proportion should be given a broader perspective. Israel allocates almost half of its budget to defense, while pre-revolutionary Portugal devoted over two-fifths to its armed forces. In Africa, in terms of gross national product, Uganda, Tanzania, and Zaire set aside a smaller proportion, while Zambia, Somalia, and Nigeria spend more on defense than South Africa does. It is also worth noting that the Republic is not yet near the limit of its capacity to finance an even greater military effort. As Edouard Bustin has commented in a perceptive essay, "It seems clear that, under escalating pressure, the government could easily mobilise a much larger proportion of its resources for military purposes."[2]

There is equally no reason to doubt the sophistication of the South African military machine's organization and equipment. In terms of training, equipment, and hitting power, it has no equal in black Africa. Like the Israelis, the South Africans maintain only a small standing army (the Permanent Force) and count principally on a conscripted army and rapid mobilization of reserves in times of crisis. Full mobilization would realize two divisions equipped with modern tanks (British Centurions), armored cars, artillery, and missiles. The navy boasts three submarines, two destroyers, five corvettes, and ten mine sweepers, with two more submarines, two frigates, three missile-firing patrol boats, and six corvettes on order, making it formidable by African standards. The air force is also relatively powerful, equipped mainly with French Mirage fighters (including a squadron of the advanced F-1), C-130 transports, and French helicopters.[3] There are early-warning systems monitoring the northern borders in the Transvaal and the most modern air and naval monitoring facility in Africa at Silvermine near Cape Town. The Simonstown naval base has the best dockyard in the south Atlantic. Adapted to meet every possible contingency, the South African Defence Force is a flexible instrument designed to cope equally with conventional warfare, counterinsurgency operations, and support for the police in the event of internal insurrection.

The main problems for the military have centered on arms supplies and manpower. Since the early 1960s when the Americans, British, and United Nations imposed their arms embargoes against the Republic, the fear of being deprived of foreign supplies has nourished a thriving domestic armament industry that meets most of the country's needs in conventional weaponry—small arms, ammunition, military vehicles, artillery—and assembles foreign-made aircraft and helicopters under license. The South African minister of defense, P.W. Botha, said in Parliament in April, 1977, that 57 percent of the country's arms requirements, including naval craft, were supplied from local sources. If ships were excluded, South Africa was self-sufficient for 75 percent of its needs. The chief concern of the military planners is with the future availability of sophisticated arms such as ships and fighter aircraft, especially if the arms boycott widens while the Republic's enemies gain greater access to weapons from Soviet and Chinese arsenals. The Angolan war, in which South African troops faced modern rockets and artillery for the first time, underscores this anxiety, as does France's declared intention of joining the ranks of the boycotters, although much of the useful weaponry already in the French pipeline will be delivered. The importance of new sources of arms is becoming vital, and Pretoria's closer ties with countries like Israel and Iran as a response to this challenge will be discussed later in this chapter.

Manpower is not yet a serious problem for the South African military, but it could be in the future if the fortress is subjected to a siege. The progressive call-up of able-bodied whites in Rhodesia, and the economic and pyschological dislocation that it has caused, point to the difficulties ahead. The Republic has a much larger white population than its neighbor and a correspondingly higher white-to-black ratio: 1 to 22 in Rhodesia, 1 to 4 in South Africa. The South African government has not inducted Africans into its forces, whereas more than half of the Rhodesian army is now black. There is a historic fear in South Africa of arming the African, and Defence Minister Botha has strongly opposed alleviating the manpower shortage by turning to the blacks. "I am not in favour of it," he said in Parliament in April, 1977, "and as long as I remain Minister of Defence it won't happen." Since the Angolan war, the Cape Coloured infantry regiment, disbanded after the Nationalists came to power in 1948, has been re-formed and has served on the Angolan border. An Indian battalion has also been recruited. Blacks are, however, entering the noncombatant service branches of the army, Bantustan infantry units are being trained, and there is a large black component in the police force. The South Africans stress their unique "commando" system: local, well-trained auxiliaries that can be called up quickly to cope with internal unrest or used for counterinsurgency in the rural areas. "Womanpower" is another resource taken seriously by military planners, who point to the role women played in industry and offices during the Second World War and are now playing in Rhodesia.* Nevertheless, there is no denying that the need for manpower is increasing. A call for volunteers by the government has not been very successful, and in April, 1977, the period of conscription was increased from one to two years. Since whites hold nearly all the skilled jobs, any large mobilization is bound to have a damaging effect on the economy, although it would also mean, as it did during the Second World War, that Africans would advance more quickly up the job ladder.

The South African government has concentrated much of its energies on developing a nuclear capability. In 1974, shortly after the Portuguese coup in Lisbon, Dr. Louw Alberts, vice-president of South Africa's Atomic Energy Board, announced, "Our technology and science have advanced sufficiently for us to produce an atomic bomb if we have to." In May, 1976, Vorster added: "We can enrich uranium, and we have the capability. And

---

* The South African minister of defense announced at the end of 1976 that women would be trained for noncombat duties in the army and commandos.

we did not sign the nuclear non-proliferation treaty." South Africa is thus in the "near-nuclear" league but will probably pause there with the aim of deterring its African enemies and warning its Western friends rather than going on to develop its technology to the point of exploding an atomic device. For the moment, its conventional forces are adequate to deal with conventional threats; any further advance in its nuclear capability is likely to be counterproductive, since it could have the effect of encouraging the more advanced African countries to develop their own atomic weapons.

There are, moreover, the deterring effects of delivery and cost. As Edouard Bustin has written, "The mere possession of a nuclear device cannot be separated from the problem of its delivery." He quotes M. Hough, a South African political scientist, on the subject: "It serves no purpose to manufacture a bomb in a military vacuum in the hope that either the prestige or fear associated with it will make it worth the effort."[4] Bustin concludes:

> Since we are ultimately dealing with a problem of credibility, it
> might be argued that whatever bargaining advantage Pretoria
> might be able to spin off from the exercise of its nuclear options
> could be derived more effectively (and is indeed already being
> derived) from publicizing its capacity to "go nuclear"—which is
> highly credible—rather than from the threat of subsequently
> using such weapons—which is demonstrably less credible.[5]

The cost of going nuclear is another braking factor, especially in view of the straitened circumstances of the South African economy and the heavy demands made upon it by other pressing priorities.

Nuclear power for peaceful purposes is an important part of the drive for self-sufficiency in energy, and Pretoria is unlikely to spoil its chances for securing the technology it needs in this field by an aggressive posture on nuclear weapons. It is equally unlikely to sign the nuclear nonproliferation treaty because it wants to maintain maximum flexibility in its defense strategy.

South Africa is the industrial colossus of the continent. With 4 percent of the land area and 6 percent of the population, South Africa generates 40 percent of Africa's industrial production, accounts for 45 percent of its mineral output, owns 50 percent of its vehicles, and absorbs half of the continent's foreign investment.[6] Since the early 1960s, the Republic has maintained a high rate of real economic growth (7-8 percent per annum between 1963 and 1973), putting it in the same league as Japan and Brazil. It has sophisticated road, railway, port, and aeronautical and communications systems.

South Africans pride themselves on their free-enterprise economy. Capitalism is regarded as part of their Western heritage, a system that permits them to prosper and share their natural riches, at mutual profit, with the rest of the world. In fact, South Africa has never enjoyed a free economy because its racial policies have always strictly controlled the use of labor and the siting of business. Since the Sharpeville shootings in 1960, when capital fled the country, the government has exercised an increasingly tight rein. With a siege mentality developing, the bit has gouged ever deeper as Pretoria shows a greater determination to channel economic resources into crucial areas to strengthen the state against the hostile forces around it. Noting the trend, an analyst, in a May 1, 1976, *Forbes* magazine article, reported, "South Africa is an authoritarian society and a partly socialist one as well. The government owns the major steel company, oil refineries, chemical plants, railroads, the airline, coal processors, electric utilities and communications. The step toward a fully statist society would not be such a great one—and with survival at stake, might not be greatly resisted by the bulk of the whites." In an editorial at the beginning of 1977, South Africa's leading economic journal, the *Financial Mail,* commented, "A survey of the known portion of 1977's legislative programme confirms the familiar Vorster pattern of increased State control over the private sector."

Facts to support that prediction are not hard to find. Measures to ban strikes—by whites, that is; black strikes were already illegal—to expand the emergency powers of the armed forces, to requisition civilian buildings and transport, and to force banks, insurance companies, and pension funds to invest a larger percentage of their funds in government bonds have been introduced. Belt-tightening fiscal measures designed to reduce the country's balance-of-payments deficit and its reliance on fuel imports featured strongly in the 1977-78 budget. A protectionist barrier has been thrown up with a 15 percent surcharge on imports as the country sinks into the trough of the recession which hit South Africa later than it did the Western industrialized countries. The government has warned the whites that they can no longer expect automatic increases in their affluent standard of living as inflation continues at the rate of 11 percent, unemployment grows alarmingly, and real growth hovers a little above the zero mark.

But these are tactical measures. What most concerns the South African government are the long-term strategic vulnerabilities: the problems of oil, gold, foreign capital, and growth. Economic strength and self-reliance are clearly important facets of Pretoria's "total strategy," and although neither can be divorced from political developments, the government is doggedly pursuing these goals. Any form of economic boycott is anathema because South Africa is a trading nation dependent on the outside world for many essential items. Of these, the most vital is its energy supply, especially oil.

The sources of South Africa's energy are coal (73 percent), imported crude oil (21 percent), hydroelectric power (3 percent), and oil from coal, produced by the government-run SASOL plant (3 percent). The Republic has abundant supplies of coal and is becoming a major exporter; its only deficiency is coking coal, necessary for smelting, and extensive exploration is going on in the northern Transvaal in an effort to replace the large amounts that are currently imported. Nuclear energy is being developed but is unlikely to have a significant impact on the overall energy situation in the foreseeable future. Moreover, the principal economic function of the South African nuclear program is the acquisition of foreign exchange through the sale of enriched fuels rather than self-sufficiency in electricity. Hydroelectric power from the Cabora-Bassa Dam in Mozambique is now on stream after many delays, but the government has made it clear that, for political reasons, it will not allow itself to become too dependent on that source. The dam provides 3 percent of the Republic's electricity needs; this percentage will increase over the next three years but not beyond the level of 7 percent.

This leaves oil, the Achilles' heel of South Africa's strategic planners. There are two sources of anxiety: its availability, threatened by embargoes and cartels, and its cost, which knocks a jagged hole in the country's foreign exchange earnings. South Africa is almost totally dependent on Iran for its crude oil needs, estimated to be between 300,000 and 350,000 barrels a day.* The link with the shah—historic, economic, and strategic—is secure for the moment, but no government in Pretoria's isolated position can be entirely happy with such an exposed and one-sided dependence. The Republic has no oil of its own apart from the small amount produced by the SASOL process. It has been exploring on a large scale since 1966 but without success. An extra effort is being made with a $150-million exploration program in the offshore areas near the Western Cape. Exploration in South-West Africa has waned following disappointing results and the uncertain political situation. Although oil-bearing rock formations have been located, the prospects for finding large quantities of oil in or near South Africa are not good. But this has not deterred the South Africans from continuing the quest, and it is perhaps significant that the government is prepared to invest $150 million in exploration—the annual cost has been running at a little more than $50 million—at a time when it is hard pressed by other financial considerations.

One of those considerations is also related to the availabiltiy of oil. SASOL II, the second oil-from-coal plant, which is being built in the eastern Transvaal, will probably have cost in the region of $3 billion by the time it is completed in 1980. With the smaller SASOL I plant, it is expected to provide about 40 percent of the Republic's oil requirements. Forty percent is the figure prescribed by conventional wisdom in South Africa. However, an article in the Johannesburg *Financial Mail* on December 10, 1976, challenged the figure, arguing that "at today's level of demand [SASOL II's]

---

* On April 18, 1975, the Johannesburg *Financial Mail* reported: "Industry sources confirm that South Africa is now overwhelmingly (about 90%) at the mercy of Iran for its crude oil supplies, with the balance coming largely from Iraq and Indonesia." The percentage from Iran may have increased since then.

production would account for just less than 35% of the domestic petrol market. By 1982, though, the market share will have fallen to between 25% and 28%." The two SASOLs will also save approximately $460 million a year in foreign exchange at 1977 oil prices, a reduction of more than a third of the total oil bill. That, for the South African government, is the good news. Less cheering is the problem of meeting SASOL II's soaring cost and the fact that even when the plant is on stream, South Africa will remain dependent on outsiders for almost two-thirds of its oil.

The main sources of financing for SASOL II are the government's Strategic Oil Fund, parliamentary allocations, and foreign loans. The Strategic Oil Fund, which draws its resources from a consumers' gasoline levy, was specially created to finance SASOL II and the country's oil reserve (a "stockpool" rather than a stockpile). Large sums are regularly paid into this fund, and a breakdown given in the South African Parliament in mid-1976 indicated how this money is used. The minister of economic affairs reported that $180 million had been paid into the fund as of April 30, 1976. Seventy-one million had gone into construction costs of SASOL II; $89.6 million had been used on "investment for SASOL II"; and $17.8 million had been set aside for oil stockpooling and fighting pollution. Many critics of the SASOL scheme in South Africa argue that its cost—80 percent of which will be met from internal resources—is already crippling and shows signs of spiraling even higher. The government counters by saying that the 20 percent slice of foreign capital will be repaid within two years of SASOL II's going into operation by foreign exchange savings on the oil-import bill. The managing director of the project, Johannes Stegmann, is adamant that it should not and cannot be scrapped. In a December, 1976, Johannesburg *Financial Mail* interview, he said: "We conceived the project with one eye on our strategic situation and the other on our balance of payments. They're both as critical as ever." While serious doubts remain about SASOL II's economic viability, the threats of oil embargoes and the increasing price of oil add weight to the strategic and balance-of-payments arguments. And of these two, the strategic factor is the one that counts most with the South African government.

The cost of imported oil is the other major source of concern to South Africa's strategic planners. The import bill has risen from $270 million in 1972 to $1.38 billion in 1976. With OPEC's 10 percent price rise in early 1977 and the increase in domestic consumption, the cost is expected to rise steadily. The government has taken a number of measures to curb consumption. Gas stations are closed on weekends; the speed limit throughout the country has been lowered and is enforced by heavy fines; and there are moves to make the recycling of oil waste compulsory. There have been pressures on the government to use some of its oil reserves, but these have been resisted, once again for strategic reasons. The oil stockpool, stored underground in different parts of the country, is estimated to be sufficient to supply the country's needs, at peacetime rates of consumption, for about two years.

Gold is another of South Africa's strategic vulnerabilities, for, like oil, the government depends upon it for survival; like oil too, its fate is not fully in South African hands but subject to whims and forces beyond Pretoria's control. For generations South Africans have agreed with Christopher Columbus that "gold is a metal most excellent above others and of gold treasures are formed, and he who has it makes and accomplishes whatever he wishes in the world." Belief in gold, like belief in one's country, has been a simple and natural act of faith. When the gold price soared to $200 an ounce in 1974, it was exciting but somehow regarded as part of the inevitable order of things. Two years later the price had slumped to $104 an ounce. Since then, although the price has increased and has settled close to midway between those two extremes, South Africans' blind faith in the yellow metal has been shaken and its excellence can no longer be accepted unquestioningly.

Gold accounts for 40 percent of the Republic's foreign exchange earnings and 75 percent of the Western world's production. But gold output is diminishing in South Africa as a result of depleted reserves and rising costs. The future holds little hope of a reversal of this trend. M.D.A. Etheredge, head of the gold-mining division of the giant Anglo-American Corporation, put it this way: "Gold production in South Africa is on the last plateau before the long decline." Output will be between 700 and 800 tons annually for the next decade, Etheredge said, but unless there is a spectacular rise in the gold price or a discovery of an entirely new gold field—both "remote" possibilities—"our gold production will fall quite rapidly after 1986. At the turn of this century it is likely to be only half of what it is now." In 1974 gold sales produced $3.2 billion in foreign currency; in 1975, $2.9 billion; and in 1976 the figure was down to $2.5 billion. Fluctuations in the world price of the metal have a disturbing effect on the South African economy. Every rise of $10 an ounce in the price of gold produces, over a year, an additional $230 million in foreign currency. Conversely, every drop of $10 depletes the country's reserves by the same amount, or, put another way, by $4.4 million a week. In the opinion of the Johannesburg *Financial Mail*, gold will continue to provide an essential base for the economy worth around $2.5 billion a year. "It will not, however, provide any significant growth above that." To put this figure into proportion, it is worth noting that South Africa has allocated $1.9 billion for its defense in the 1977-78 budget and that its oil bill for 1976 was $1.38 billion.

The two factors that have had the greatest effect on the price of gold are both external. The first might be called the panic impulse, which has operated during times of inflation and uncertainty, as in the wake of the Arab oil embargo and fourfold oil price rise in 1973-74, when governments and individuals rushed to buy gold, thus pushing up the price. The second was the International Monetary Fund's new policy of regular gold auctions for the benefit of the world's poorer countries, a policy strongly backed by the United States in its drive to demonetize gold. The fund's sales began in the summer of 1976 and will continue until 1980. They could not have come at a worse time for the South African government (the Soweto riots broke out two weeks after the first auction), and although the gold price has stabilized at about $150 an ounce and seems less responsive to the regular monthly sales, the South Africans are acutely aware of their vulnerability to forces over which they have very little control.

In late 1976 a South African official in Pretoria, admitting that the year had been one of unmitigated disaster, asked me to guess what the worst setback had been. I tried Angola, Soweto, and, finally, the economic recession. He shook his head. "None of those," he said. "It was William Simon, secretary of the United States Treasury, South Africa's public enemy number one." It seems that the United States has, almost inadvertently, acquired economic leverage over the South African government through its gold policy and the influence it can bring to bear in world councils on the price and monetary role of that precious commodity. This influence also, of course, played a part in the abolition of the official price of gold in early 1975, a move which encouraged holders of gold to sell and contributed to the rapid decline in the world price. American leverage is further enhanced by the fact that when the gold price sinks, the South African government invariably turns to the American banks for loans to plug the deficit.

The drop in the gold price has had several effects on the Republic. A number of gold mines have been pushed to the brink of closure; many others are in the marginal category as costs have outstripped revenue. The halcyon days when gold was king have gone, and with them the illusion of power and an untrammeled vision of the future. Graham Hatton, now editor of the *Financial Mail,* described what has happened in an article in the July 23, 1976, London *Financial Times.*

> In 1974 and 1975 the government became the victim of its
> own pro-gold propaganda and boosted state expenditure levels
> accordingly. At the end of 1974, when gold was at its peak, the
> Minister of Finance predicted an average of $200 an ounce in
> the period ahead. State spending in subsequent budgets
> reflected this optimism.

South Africa now has to cut its coat according to its cloth, and with the decision to revalue its gold holdings nearer to the market price, abandoning the old official rate of $42.20 an ounce, the metal has assumed a less ambiguous role in the country's economy.

Worried by the fading luster of gold, the South African government has made a conscious effort to develop its other mineral resources by digging deep into the riches that lie under its soil. In 1976 alone, two new harbors, built at great cost and with the primary intention of exporting minerals, came into operation. Including associated port and railway facilities, Richards Bay in Natal and Saldanha Bay in the Western Cape cost about $1.5 billion but will result in a significant increase in mineral exports. These produced just over $1 billion in 1975 and are expected to produce twice as much, more than $2 billion, in 1978. The minerals contributing to this bonanza are coal, iron ore, titanium, uranium, platinum, industrial diamonds, copper, and ferrochrome. The South African government is aware that the

world demand for these resources—and hence the price—is likely to be
more favorable than that of gold. If the latter's price does not rise substantially, as seems likely, mineral exports other than gold during 1977 and 1978 will probably equal gold as a foreign exchange earner and may overtake it in 1979.

There is one further benefit to be gained from putting more eggs into the mineral basket and that is the political advantage of binding the West (especially the United States, which is a large consumer of South African metals) more intimately in a state of dependence. This may be a secondary consideration for the South Africans, but it seems to be important nonetheless. According to a report prepared for the United States Department of Commerce by Charles River Associates, Inc., of Cambridge, Massachusetts, early in 1977, it was South Africa's ambition "to increase greatly, in fact eventually to dominate, the world chromite and ferrochrome markets." The Republic is the chief source of both chromite ore and ferrochrome for the United States.[7]

There is, however, a drawback to the mineral basket: a lack of eggs. Huge amounts of capital are still needed to expand production, and any growth beyond the 1978 projections will depend on the availability of foreign capital. Energy, water (especially for the new discoveries in the dry northwestern Cape), and transport infrastructure will all be needed in greater amounts. The shortage of skilled labor is another major constraint, but all these obstacles could be overcome if the money became available. Infrastructure and power would cost an estimated further $1 billion a year initially but would tail off, while another $1 billion would probably be needed for the mining and processing operations required to prepare the minerals for export. South Africa's finance secretary, Gerald Browne, confirmed the need in more general terms: "Before we will be able to generate more capital from mineral exports, we will have to spend vast amounts."[8] Whether the necessary capital materializes or not depends partly on the political situation inside South Africa and partly on the willingness of Western financial institutions and companies to continue bankrolling the industry. There is no doubt that the latter have played a key role in developing the Republic's mineral wealth. Analyzing the state of the industry in late 1976, the *Financial Time's* South African correspondent wrote, "These [mining] projects have generally been notable for the way many have been joint ventures between local mining groups and major multinational concerns, particularly from the United States, involving mining, industrial and oil companies."

The need for foreign capital, especially medium- and long-term financing, raises the third critical area of vulnerability in South Africa's economic defenses. To maintain a growth rate sufficient to absorb the swelling ranks of the black labor force and hence ensure political stability, South Africa needs a steady input of skilled labor—white immigration, in effect—and massive injections of capital. The immigrants are still coming in, though no longer at the rate of 30,000 (net) a year projected by the economic planners. The minerals industry is especially concerned about the shortage of skilled labor. A former Minerals Bureau deputy director has pointed out that "labour, particularly skilled and professional labour, looms as the major constraint to the development of the minerals industry."[9] Short-term loans, up to five years, are still obtainable, but interest rates have increased and since the Angolan war and the black upheavals in 1976, South Africa has usually had to pay a premium of at least 1.5 percent over the London Interbank Offered Rate for foreign loans. Large sums were borrowed to bolster the Republic's sagging gold and foreign reserves, which plummeted from nearly $1.4 billion in April, 1976, to $800 million four months later. The reserves have since received a boost from drawings on the International Monetary Fund and through the abandonment of the official gold price, which has meant that the gold element in the reserves (roughly half of the total) has more than trebled in value. But South Africa's continuing difficulties, even over short-term loans, are illustrated by the time it took to secure a five-year, $110-million syndicated Eurodollar loan in late 1976 and by the fact that the minister of finance, in his 1977-78 budget, concluded that the borrowing needed for the next year would have to come from local sources. Things may improve as the balance-of-payments deficit is reduced and if the world economic recovery, led by the United States, continues steadily.

The real problem, however, is long-term borrowing, and it is in this sphere that South Africa is at the mercy of the industrialized powers. According to *Business Week* (April 18, 1977), "New foreign investment [in South Africa] has virtually dried up." The attitude of foreign investors is not total rejection but rather wait-and-see, and their caution is the result of straightforward economic factors as well as of concern about the political uncertainties of the region. According to the *Wall Street Journal,* the net inflow of foreign capital to South Africa declined from $1.9 billion in 1975 to $1.1 billion in 1976. Apart from affecting the government's finances, the diminishing flow of foreign money has caused problems for the country's ambitious development projects. The state-controlled South African steel producer, ISCOR, confirmed in late 1976 that a shortage of capital in the "international and South African markets" had resulted in the shelving of plans to build a steel processing plant at Saldanha Bay. To secure existing investments, the government has shored up its defenses by progressively reducing foreign holdings in the country's commercial banks, by instituting tougher exchange controls, and by introducing a measure to prevent foreign companies from repatriating profits earned prior to January, 1975. As the siege tightens, it seems likely that the problem of foreign capital—more than oil or gold—will cause the defenders of fortress South Africa the greatest anxiety.

South Africa's drive for greater military and economic strength has led it beyond the continent of Africa in a search for new allies. The recipients of

Pretoria's advances have usually been nations that not only find themselves in a similarly isolated international position but that also share a sense of uneasiness about their relationships with the Western powers. Israel and Iran are the most important, but closer relations have also been fostered with Taiwan, South Korea, Paraguay, Uruguay, and Chile. The phenomenon has been variously dubbed the pariahs' club, the alliance of the disenchanted, and, somewhat melodramatically, the league of the desperate. The grouping may be loose and ephemeral—its basic objectives are tactical rather than strategic—but it merits attention because most of the countries involved possess a respectable military capability, some mastery of modern technology (South Africa, Israel, and Iran are "threshold" nuclear powers), and potential leverage in terms of vital resources or strategic locations. They view themselves as "middle-level" powers, strongly anticommunist, nonaggressive, internally stable, and devotedly loyal to the Western alliance. Their individual motives for closer links with each other vary, but most of them feel that their unswerving friendship with the United States and Western Europe has not been properly rewarded and that the isolation they suffer from has been unfairly thrust upon them. In such circumstances they see no harm in turning their backs on the world community and showing the West that they have minds of their own. South Africa is the most active member of the pariahs' club, perhaps because it is also the most isolated. And it is the nexus with Israel that has aroused the greatest controversy.

The countries are no strangers to each other, for their relationship has deep historical roots. The Zionist movement opened an office in Johannesburg as early as 1898, and in 1917 General Jan Smuts, the minister of defense in the Union government, helped to draft the Balfour Declaration. Successive South African governments supported Zionist aspirations in Palestine, and Daniel Malan, the first leader of a Nationalist administration, recognized Israel in 1948 and later visited the country. Relations remained friendly but not particularly close during the 1950s and 1960s when Israel sought to woo black Africa and when South Africa endeavoured to promote its contacts with the Arab nations. Israel had established a legation in Pretoria and a consulate-general in Johannesburg shortly after independence, but South Africa chose to be represented through Britain as a member of the Commonwealth until the break with that organization in 1961. South Africa was not formally represented in the Jewish state for the next decade, the beginning and end of which witnessed the two lowest points in their relations. In 1962 Pretoria blocked the transfer of Zionist funds to Israel in retaliation for the latter's alignment with the African states in their assault on apartheid in the United Nations. Israel even went as far as to vote for the use of sanctions against the Republic. The 1967 war, however, brought a surge of popular support for Israel among white South Africans, and Pretoria acted quickly to facilitate a flow of funds, materials, and volunteers to Tel Aviv.

At about this time a growing identity of interest between the two countries was recognized in National party circles in South Africa, best summed up perhaps in a May 29, 1968, editorial in *Die Burger*, the party's newspaper in Cape Province.

> Israel and South Africa have a common lot. Both are engaged
> in a struggle for existence, and both are in a constant clash with
> the decisive majorities in the United Nations. Both are reliable
> foci of strength within the region which would, without them,
> fall into anti-Western anarchy.... The anti-Western powers
> have driven Israel and South Africa into a community of in-
> terests which had better be utilised than denied.

Israel, however, was steadily pursuing its policy of friendship and cooperation with black Africa, a target deemed of greater importance than a closer
embrace with the apartheid Republic, which, though well-disposed toward
Israel, seemed geographically remote and politically isolated. By the early
1970s, Israel had established diplomatic relations with thirty-two African
countries and had resident missions in sixteen of them. South African-Israeli relations plummeted for the second time in 1971, when Pretoria pro-
tested strongly after the Israeli government had offered $5,000 worth of
food, medicine, and blankets to the Organization of African Unity's assistance fund for the liberation movements. The South African government
again blocked Zionist funds until Israel hurriedly withdrew its offer, and relations remained cool until the 1973 Middle East war.

Throughout most of that period, South Africa was the wooer and Israel the wooed. The reasons are not hard to find. There are only 120,000
Jews in the Republic (out of a white population of 4.3 million), but they
form one of the most effective of all Zionist lobbies, contributing more per
capita than any other national group in the world and ranking second only
to American Jewry in total annual contributions to Israel. The Jewish
community in South Africa is rich, powerful in commerce and industry,
and, on the whole, conformist, although some of the government's most
outspoken critics are Jews. There used to be some antisemitism in the National party, but this has been gradually whittled away and is no longer of
any political significance, although the sight of Prime Minister Vorster paying hommage at Jewish shrines in Israel during his visit in April, 1976,
probably raised a few skeptical eyebrows out in the *platteland.* (Conservative Afrikaners, however, were by this stage becoming used to their prime
minister's traveling to outlandish places and meeting unlikely people. Only
six months before, Vorster had shaken hands with President Kaunda of
Zambia in a railway carriage over the Victoria Falls.)

A second reason for South Africa's ardor was its declining fortunes
with the Arabs. Egypt had broken off relations with the Republic in 1961,
and the group of North African Arabs in the Organization of African Unity
tended to raise the level of militancy toward South Africa in the Arab world
in general. South Africa had, in the past, received a small percentage of its
oil from Arab exporters, and this had encouraged a certain amount of self-
restraint in its overtures to Israel. But as Vorster gained confidence in inter-

national affairs, it seems clear that he felt he could take the calculated risk of moving closer to Israel without offending his Arab oil suppliers. The steadfastness of Iran, another pariah power, as South Africa's principal source of oil further encouraged Pretoria to pursue its outward policy with the Israelis.

The October war marked a decisive turning point in the relationship, as Israel's African policy collapsed. One by one, the black African nations broke off relations, and before long the Jewish state found itself with a sole supporter on the continent: South Africa. Since the war, Israel has either abstained, been absent from or voted against United Nations resolutions condemning South Africa. Israeli support for South Africa at the United Nations has been made easier by the Arabs' ill-judged Zionism-is-a-form-of-racism resolution in November, 1975. Israeli delegates, when abstaining from or voting against resolutions condemning racism in South Africa, say that the issue has been "contaminated" by the Arabs' linking it to Zionism. The Republic has reciprocated by not calling on Israel to withdraw from occupied Arab territory.

Since the Vorster visit, during which a pact covering technological, scientific, and trade affairs was signed, ties between the two countries have been strengthened. Israel has elevated its diplomatic mission in Pretoria to embassy status, appointing an ambassador who speaks fluent Afrikaans, and a South African ambassador has gone to Tel Aviv. Trade has quadrupled since 1972 and was worth about $100 million in 1976. The commodities exchanged reveal the complementary nature of the two countries' needs. South Africa's main exports include raw diamonds, steel, cement, timber, and sugar, with coal expected to be a major item in the future. In return, Israel sells chemicals, textiles, pharmaceuticals, electronic equipment, and machinery to the Republic and processes the diamonds for re-export. *
In 1975 South Africa was designated a preferred export target by the Israeli Ministry of Trade and Industry, a status that gives exporters special incentives. Bilateral enterprises have been initiated, the most important being a joint steel project by the two state-controlled industries, through which South Africa supplies Israel with 25 percent of its steel requirements; Israeli participation in a South African electronics factory near Pretoria; and a massive ten-year coal-export deal that will help reduce Israel's dependence on oil by providing about three million tons of coal annually for a giant power station under construction near Hadera in central Israel. In a special concession to South African Jews, Pretoria has allowed its citizens to invest in Israel up to an annual limit of $25 million. A former Israeli consul-general to South Africa summed up the prospects recently: "With South Africa's abundance of raw materials, and Israel's know-how, we can really go places if we join forces."

The military component of the relationship is the most tantalizing and the most subterranean. In February, 1976, two months before Vorster's

---

* The Israeli diamond-polishing industry earns about $500 million annually, about 40 percent of the country's export earnings.

visit to Israel, an agreement to sell South Africa three long-range gunboats of the Reshef class with Gabriel guided missile systems was signed. Later reports suggested that the number had risen to six and that South African naval personnel had gone to Haifa for training. According to another report, South Africa is making the armor for the new Israeli tank, the Ben Gurion, but beyond this there is no hard evidence of a more elaborate military connection, although there is much speculation about Israel's desire to find new markets for its burgeoning arms industry and about South Africa's need to circumvent the arms embargo. Israel is particularly eager to sell its new fighter-bomber, the Kfir (literally, "lion cub" in Hebrew but embarrassingly similar to *kaffir,* a derogatory term for blacks in South Africa). South Africa already has Mirage fighters, from which the Kfir was developed, and needs a new combat aircraft of the Israeli plane's caliber. Vorster made a point of visiting a Kfir factory when he was in Israel, but so far there has been no sign of a sale. The main obstacle is that the Kfir is fitted with American-made General Electric J-79 engines, and formal permission must be granted by Washington before Israel can sell the aircraft to a third party. The United States government blocked the sale of several Kfirs to Ecuador in February, 1977—although it permitted a sale to Austria three months later—and it is highly unlikely that it would relax the ban in the case of South Africa, a country which has been subjected to an American arms embargo since 1963. Other forms of military cooperation between South Africa and Israel are harder to monitor, but counterinsurgency techniques, border defenses, and nuclear technology are areas in which the former has many questions and the latter a number of answers. In view of the warmth of the relationship, it would be surprising if a productive dialogue had not begun.

How serious is the intention "to join forces and really go places"? The answer seems to depend upon which side is asked, the ardent South African swain or the slightly coy Israeli maiden. In the Republic, only the black nationalists question the liaison; the government and its white supporters, especially the Jewish community, back it enthusiastically and want it to flourish.* Pretoria sees no conflict between its Israeli policy and its continuing aim of dialogue in black Africa because it notes that Israel has also managed to maintain a friendly, if low-keyed, contact with several African states.**

For Israel, however, the situation is more complicated. The break with black Africa in the wake of the 1973 war was a bitter disappointment and

---

* There are a few notable exceptions, principally Jewish rabbis and intellectuals, who have publicly criticized the relationship and think Israel has made a serious mistake.

** Israel's former premier, Yitzhak Rabin, had talks with Felix Houphouet-Boigny, president of Ivory Coast and a leading proponent of dialogue with South Africa, in Geneva in February, 1977. Three African states—Malawi, Lesotho, and Swaziland, all closely linked with South Africa—still have diplomatic relations with Israel.

paved the way for a more receptive attitude toward South Africa. The Republic's own success in dealing with Africa during the Vorster-Kaunda de-
tente period may have helped to convince the Israeli government that
open friendship with the Republic would not necessarily preclude rap-
prochement with Africa later on. The common pariah feeling, reinforced by
the traditional Israeli desire to show the United States that it is not a client
state, also edged the two countries a little closer. Another consideration
was the openhandedness and devoted loyalty of South Africa's Jewish
population. There are also 7,000 settlers of South African origin in Israel,
who add political and economic weight to bilateral relations, and the South
African government not only allows generous contributions to go to Israel
but now encourages investment. Finally, the Republic's steel and coal, particularly the latter, are of considerable value to Israel at a time when it is
building a major new railway between Eilat and Beersheba and developing
coal-fired electric power plants.

But there is no doubt that the liaison has given ammunition to Israel's
enemies and provoked deep concern among its relatives and friends. The
Arabs, in their drive to maintain African support against Israel, have made
much capital out of the Jerusalem-Pretoria nexus. For many African countries which had strong reservations about breaking with Israel in the first
place and equally powerful ones about the Zionist resolution at the United
Nations in 1975, their worst fears now appear to be confirmed. Israeli defenders of the policy point out that many African—and a few Arab—states
trade with South Africa, too, and accuse the accusers of applying a double
standard. While there can be no denying that there is a measure of hypoc-
risy (Jordan once sold South Africa fifty Centurion tanks), the Africans are
mainly concerned about future trends. They are trying to reduce their links
with South Africa in an attempt to isolate the Republic until it changes its
racial policies, while Israel is doing the opposite, thus perpetuating the insti-
tutionalized racism that the Africans had always understood Israelis abhor
as much as they do themselves. They feel particularly incensed about the
gunboat sale and rumors of further arms deals at a time when France, hitherto the most egregious offender, has finally agreed to toe the line and
when the Afro-Asian bloc at the United Nations has been trying to make
the arms embargo mandatory.

In Israel itself, the policy has been opposed by African specialists in the
Foreign Ministry, by the Histadrut (Israel's trade union federation), and by
left-wing members of the Knesset. Criticism has also come from American
blacks who support Israel and from liberal Jews in the Diaspora who have
been confused by the new policy. According to a State Department official
I interviewed, the United States government made it clear to the Israelis after Vorster's visit that it thought it was not in Israel's interest to encourage
South Africa's advances and that it certainly was not in the United States'
own interest. None of this, it seems, has served to deter either party so far,
although each appears to have a different perception of the relationship.
South Africa's view expresses itself as a strategic aim to secure long-term
and powerful friends who may be able to help it in time of need. Israel's at-

titude, born of frustration and disillusion but nourished by solid economic benefits, is tactical, pragmatic, and probably more open to revision. South Africa, particularly in military matters, is the freer agent of the two. Israel's dependency upon the United States, which is unlikely to diminish, has already had a restraining influence on the alliance. When President Carter's African policy is clarified, it is improbable that the South African-Israeli link will be viewed any more favorably than it was before, and it is possible that the Israelis will take pains to soften the tone of the relationship, while not changing its substance. The new government led by Menachem Begin is thought to be more resistant to third party pressures than its predecessor, but it is probably still true that the critical determinant of the Israeli-South African relationship lies less in either Pretoria or Jerusalem than in Washington, D.C.

South Africa's ties with Iran are not so controversial but more important, since the bulk of the Republic's oil supplies come from there. An Islamic but non-Arab state, a Third World country but not a member of the nonaligned group, a developing nation with imperial dreams, Iran under the shah has an anomalous place in international politics. Iran is the third leg of the outcasts' stool, for in keeping Israel supplied with oil, it performs the same vital function that it does for South Africa. Iran ignored the Afro-Arab oil boycotts of Israel and South Africa in 1973, and the shah has made it clear that, as long as he stays in power, he will continue to provide both countries with their crude oil requirements. Speaking in Paris in April, 1974, the shah said that continued friendship with South Africa was in his country's "long-term interests," which could not be sacrificed "to profit the interests of others who sometimes act, shall we say, for emotional reasons." The president of the Iranian senate visited South Africa the following month and stressed that, unlike the Arabs, Iran would never impose an oil embargo on the Republic.

There is a historical background to the Iranian connection. The shah's father sought political asylum in South Africa during the Second World War and died there in 1944. The present shah's sister, who with her brother spent some of her youth in the Republic, unveiled a statue to their father in the garden of the house where he used to live as part of Iran's fiftieth anniversary celebration of the Pahlevi dynasty in 1976. These sentimental ties with South Africa are believed to continue to influence the shah's policies. But there are also important economic and even strategic considerations at stake. Oil is paramount, and it is significant that the Iranian contribution to South Africa's total needs has risen spectacularly, from about 25 percent before the 1973 boycott to around 90 percent of mid-1977 consumption.[10] Some of the potential fragility of this dependence has been removed by the development of joint commercial ventures, the most important being Iran's 17.5 percent share in the Natref oil refinery at Sasolburg. This is a $112-million plant, part of the oil-from-coal SASOL complex south of Johannesburg, for which Iran supplies 70 percent of the crude oil intake. Trade has increased greatly between the two countries in recent years, especially in the export of South African steel, and on at least one occasion at a crucial time—August, 1976, at the height of the black urban upheavals—Iran helped the Republic with a large short-term loan.[11]

Another area of cooperation is the nuclear field. One report in October, 1975, that Iran was to buy $700 million worth of South African uranium and would help finance a huge uranium-enrichment plant in the Republic was denied by both countries. But it is well known that Iran has embarked on an ambitious nuclear energy program and will need a steady supply of fuel and technology. The Republic is rapidly developing its large uranium ore resources and will, when its own nuclear technology has advanced, become an exporter of enriched uranium. In mid-1974 South Africa's minister of economic affairs, after a trip to Teheran, said, "I reached firm understandings with Iran on co-operation between our two governments in the field of nuclear energy."

This pattern of mutual dependency, which basically hinges on oil for uranium, suits South Africa well enough—although having become so dependent on a single source of oil must give Pretoria's planners nightmares from time to time—and apparently it does not displease the shah. He is adept at playing the game both ways by maintaining close economic links with South Africa, yet occasionally joining in anti-apartheid rhetoric and even making small financial contributions to the Organization of African Unity's liberation fund, as, for example, in June, 1974, when the Iranian ambassador to Ethiopia handed over a $5,000 check to the Organization of African Unity saying it was his country's annual contribution for "the struggle against colonialism and apartheid on the African continent." This gesture coincided with the South African minister's mid-1974 visit to Iran. But the shah also has strategic ambitions in the Indian Ocean, and this may be an additional underpinning element in his pro-South African policy. He has talked of "a kind of commonwealth of Indian Ocean littoral states," which, he says, might include South Africa but only "after the government has introduced acceptable changes in its internal policies."[12] And he has mentioned the possibility of meeting Vorster to pursue these ideas. There was talk of the South African prime minister's visiting Teheran after his Israeli trip in April, 1976, but the visit never materialized and relations between the two countries have been conducted at ministerial or ambassadorial levels as before.

In its bid to spread its international options, the South African government has cast its net wide—and come up with some odd fish. Diplomatic relations with Taiwan were raised to ambassadorial level in April, 1976, and a South African Broadcasting Corporation commentary in Johannesburg at that time noted that the two countries had one outstanding thing in common: a steadfast opposition to international communism. Trade between them is minimal, but there may be something of greater substance in the wind if a nine-day visit to Taiwan in February, 1977, by the chief of the South African army, Lieutenant General C.L. Viljoen, means anything. He talked with Nationalist Chinese military leaders and visited a number of military establishments. The implication could be that the Republic is looking for new sources of arms.

Pretoria has cordial relations with other members of the league of the disenchanted, among them South Korea, Uruguay, and Paraguay. Vorster made state visits to the two South American republics in 1975, and South Africa has invested small but not insignificant sums in those and other Latin American countries. A Uruguayan general in full military uniform appeared at the Transkei's independence celebrations in October, 1976, the only foreign dignitary to attend. Diplomatic relations exist between South Africa and several other Latin American countries, notably Brazil, Argentina, and Chile. Brazil, with its wealth and thirst for technology, has been a special focus of South African diplomacy and, incidentally, of South Africans leaving their homeland to make a fresh start in the New World. Pretoria has invested an unspecified sum in the giant Itaipu dam on the border with Paraguay, and there are rumors of South African interest in obtaining regular supplies of oil from Venezuela.

In its African landscape, South Africa looms forbiddingly, a seemingly impregnable fortress. Yet the walls are not as thick as they look, although in the short term, the ramparts are unlikely to be breached. Beyond the immediate future, however, South Africa's inherent weaknesses are likely to prove more critical, for despite the government's determined efforts to strengthen the country, it remains vulnerable to outside pressures and forces. The West is turning away. President Carter's government has made it clear that the United States will not come to the rescue of the whites if the Nationalists continue their apartheid policies. South Africans, Vice-President Walter Mondale said after his meeting with Voster in Vienna in May, 1977, should not entertain the "illusion" that the Untied States "will, in the end, intervene to save South Africa from the policies it is pursuing, for we will not do so." Britain, France, and Germany are unlikely to act as American surrogates, although they will continue trading with and investing in South Africa. The Republic is indeed the economic giant of Africa, but on the international scale it lacks stature. In terms of population and resources, it is comparable to Canada, but its gross national product in 1975 was only $29.6 billion, less than a fifth that of Canada. An analysis of South African economic realities published in *Forbes* magazine May 1, 1976, concluded that "legend to the contrary, South Africa is not a rich country—at least not yet. Its gold mines function profitably only with dirt-cheap labor. Its industry is not competitive on a world scale. Its economy is too small to provide the capital needed to develop its great mineral resources,... and if white South Africans are well off, it is because the blacks are poor, not because the country is rich."

    The key economic vulnerabilities will continue to be oil, gold, and foreign capital, and it seems that the last of these may prove the most critical because money is the most sensitive of the three to economic and political pressures. Enemies of the Republic will look covetously at the oil and gold levers—undoubtedly the two most calculated to bring the government to its knees—but in practical terms it is difficult to imagine how they could be pulled. The shah shows no sign of wanting to end his profitable relationship with the Republic, and even if he did, other suppliers would almost certainly step into the breach. The United States has influence with the shah but probably not enough to change his mind. There is equally no sign of an end to the part gold plays in the international monetary system, or to a significant lowering of its intrinsic value on the world market. But loans, credits, and investments are inherently susceptible to the economic climate of an area and they can also be influenced by the policies of national governments. Foreign money is needed in all the vital sectors of the South African economy: to develop its mineral resources (themselves an important source of foreign exchange); to finance the balance-of-payments deficit; to buy sophisticated arms that it cannot produce itself; to purchase oil; to develop industrial infrastructure; to finance strategic resources such as the oil-from-coal process and nuclear energy and fuels. Overall, foreign capital is needed to ensure that South Africa continues to grow steadily; without that growth, apartheid and ultimately white rule itself are placed in jeopardy.

South Africa's new friends have yet to be put to the test. Israel's Likud-dominated government may resist pressure from the United States to loosen its ties with the Republic, but there seems to be a good chance that Washington will not give up trying, especially if it begins to implement its threat of adopting a posture of diplomatic hostility toward Pretoria. One of South Africa's principal aims is to obtain arms that are denied to it by the West, and it is possible it may be rewarded in places like Iran, Taiwan, and South Korea as it has already been with its shopping expedition in Israel. Some of the wealthier pariahs may also be able to provide loans—as Iran has done—or make further mutually profitable trade and barter deals. Israel can help considerably in the field of technology, and the South African government will endeavor to initiate more bilateral industrial enterprises to cement what are fundamentally relationships of tactical convenience. But it is difficult to imagine this phenomenon materially altering South Africa's fundamental dependence on the West. The Western orientation has been too broad and too all-pervasive for it to be disrupted easily. It has also been part of the white South African's innermost belief, the concept of his being a Western man—and that may be the hardest bond of all to break.

CHAPTER V

The Road Ahead

On the chessboard of South African politics, it is late in the middle game. Black is on the defensive, one or two important pieces have been lost, a few more isolated, and the pawns scattered but still numerous. White is attacking strongly, its pieces for the most part supporting each other, although there is weakness on the extreme right and left of center. A grand master casting a glance over the board would note the heavy defense of the white king and the great inferiority in the ratio of white to black pawns. He would conclude before passing on that white held the advantage but that with time black might force a draw or, if his pawns are marshaled correctly, eventually sweep across the board, turning defeat into victory.

Any number of political soothsayers' reputations are now in shreds as a result of predicting impending revolution in South Africa. But it would seem to me that something important has happened in the Republic and that the human chess game has entered a new and sustained critical phase. In the white *laager,* complacency has been replaced by a sense of foreboding; illusions of endless time and impregnable security are fading fast. In the black ghettos there is a quickening of the spirit, an understanding that there has been a qualitative change in the tempo of political life since the students' revolt in Soweto, and a feeling that time is no longer on the side of the white man. That perception is shared—though not admitted—by many realists in the government, which helps to explain why the purchase of that elusive commodity is the central aim of Pretoria's strategy. But time for what? It is sometimes said that the Afrikaner thinks of the future only in terms of a single generation, twenty years or so; he does his duty, then it is left to his sons to secure the survival of the *volk.* True or not, there is a marked immobility in Vorster and his peers, now entering their sixties, and an equally pronounced anxiety among those in their forties, the age group in which virtually all the leading *verligtes* and radicals are found. The younger generation of Afrikaners is only partially engaged, shielded by privilege, by affluence, and by a powerful and paternalistic leadership.

In contrast, the Africans, deprived of their traditional leaders or finding them inadequate, have spawned a youthful consciousness, cultural and

115

political, which is showing impatience with the failure to secure quick victories but which can afford to wait for slower ones. By the year 2000, a generation hence, Africans will outnumber whites by five to one—the ratio is currently four to one—and the black children who faced police bullets in their school blazers, waving their placards in those cold June days in 1976, will only be in their late thirties or early forties. In 2020, before they reach their sixties, the demographic surge will have lifted them into the position of outnumbering the whites by seven to one, and the latter's proportion of the total population will have sunk from 16.7 percent in 1975 to 11.3 percent in the year 2020.

The government, however, is focusing on a much shorter time span, perhaps only a decade, if indeed that. During that period it hopes to see a peaceful and acceptable evolution of black-ruled states in Rhodesia and South-West Africa, more Bantustans becoming independent, a resurgent economy, better relations with black Africa and the West, and acceptance by the steadily increasing number of nonwhites of the roles allotted to them under a modified, but not radically changed, separate-development policy. The means will be the full and ruthless utilization of the government's formidable physical power, centralized authority, and unbending will. Beyond the next decade, the government seems to have little idea of what might happen or where it is going but argues that by then priorities and attitudes may have changed so much that further modifications of apartheid, judged radical today, may be permissible. Some supporters of the system believe that it may eventually be possible to scrap it altogether if the races have learned to live in harmony without "friction." The assumption is that as apartheid evolves, the racial fears it is designed to curb will gradually fade.

"We know of no great revolution which might not have been prevented by compromise early and graciously made," Thomas Babington Macaulay, the British historian, wrote in 1828. Many people of all races in South Africa unconsciously echo his thoughts when they say the time has come for meaningful change in their society. But how much time is there? How long before the process of evolution is overtaken and swallowed by revolution? Estimates from the South African government and its critics vary, but—surprisingly—not very much. Two to five years is the consensus. Assuming the longer time-span, the last segments of the white buffer zone will have turned black; Vorster, barring ill health or accident, is likely to head the government for at least half, possibly more, of the period; and Jimmy Carter will in all probability still be in the White House when it is over and the day of reckoning arrives.

The vehicle of Afrikaner nationalism, the National party, has been in power for thirty years. It has increased its majority steadily at every election since 1948, placing it in a position of unchallengeable authority, and within it Vorster is its unchallenged leader. Yet the black students' revolt, with lim- ited, even parochial, objectives when it began on June 16, 1976, has turned into a challenge not only to the totality of government policy but to the basis on which its authority rests. The upheavals confirmed one signifi- cant trend and revealed another. They demonstrated how politicized blacks, especially the younger generation, had become; and they showed that a polarization of forces, distancing white from white, black from black, and both groups from each other, was taking place. Those two trends will be of critical importance over the next five years or so because black politi- cization will determine the strength of black pressures and the general pol- arization will determine whether those pressures express themselves in an evolutionary or revolutionary form.

The two poles are clearly defined. On the white Right there are Vor- ster and the bulk of the National party. They share the dawning realization of most whites who raise their eyes beyond the sculpted hedges of their suburban gardens that South Africa is becoming dangerously isolated in the world. But they do not draw the inference that many in the middle ground do: that the Republic's racial policies are at the root of this isolation and must be radically changed. In his 1977 New Year's speech, Vorster declared that South Africa, in the event of a communist onslaught, would stand alone and would not be able to count on arms supplies from abroad. Stitching together various statements made by the prime minister in the second half of 1976 as the black townships erupted and burned, the Jo- hannesburg *Financial Mail* (April 22, 1977) came to the conclusion that Vorster was as strongly committed as ever to the fundamentals of apart- heid; he had finished talking about political rights; he would investigate "shortcomings" in separate development but would go no further; there would be no urban Africans alongside Coloureds and Indians on the Cab- inet Councils; urban Africans had to exercise their political rights in the Bantustans; there would be no national convention since its aim would be to tear up the constitution and replace it with one man, one vote. In other words, the *Financial Mail* concluded, "The denial to Africans in the cities of political rights where they live and work is now part of the organic law of the country, an accomplished, irreversible fact."

At the other pole, the black Left is equally uncompromising. The black consciousness and nationalist movements want the apartheid structures dismantled and full political rights granted to all South Africans in a united country: in short, majority rule. They offer no special protection for minor- ities apart from a universal bill of rights, but they acknowledge that groups such as the whites and the Indians would continue to wield disproportion- ate influence through their skills and economic power. They oppose fed- eralism, confederalism, and partition. The nationalist movements have al- ready adopted a revolutionary posture and the radical youth are close to doing so. Black leaders would agree to sit around a table and talk to their white rulers, to discuss ways and means and timetables for the dismantling of apartheid, but no one has asked them yet. Nor, in the five-year period under discussion, are they likely to be asked. Dialogue will be feasible only when the power equation is more evenly balanced, as eventually occurred in Rhodesia and South-West Africa, which means a net loss of white power and a net gain of black. Meanwhile, the struggle is for the middle ground.

But first, is there such a thing as a middle ground in South African politics? And second, if there is, what purpose can it serve if those implacable white and black polarities are exerting such a magnetic attraction?

The middle ground is there and is important. South African society is only just beginning to feel the reverberations of the storm that is approaching. While it is true that fragments from the center are being pulled to one extreme or the other, the process of polarization is also dividing the racial groups among themselves, perhaps only temporarily but long enough to leave a fluid and crowded situation in the center. A leading South African journalist, Stanley Uys, wrote in the *New Statesman* (December 13, 1974), "There is a vast mass of white and black South Africans who don't know what to think and who spend their lives, as someone put it recently, riding the roller-coaster of hope and foreboding." There is still much truth in that view, despite the traumas of the intervening period.

The middle ground is especially important because it provides a focus for Western policy-makers. This is not to say the middle ground itself is a force, a viable alternative to the might of Afrikaner and African nationalisms. It is not. But it could provide an evolutionary mechanism, of necessity a transitional device, when power between the two major forces is more evenly balanced. The use of the middle ground, peopled by black and white moderates, will also appeal to the leaders of the African frontline states, who, as material supporters of South African black power, will inevitably become involved in the crisis.

The middle ground is, therefore, a forum and a focus rather than a fulcrum. It has some power of its own but it can be effective only if the real forces in the land choose to use it. However, South Africa's industrial base and complex economy endow the center with more inherent strength than is found in rural Rhodesia or South-West Africa, where politics, especially white politics, are conducted largely at the level of the village pump. But there is great confusion and uncertainty. A critic of the South African government once described its sports policy as resembling a centipede out of step with itself. In the wake of the black students' revolt, this image reflects the state of political forces in the middle ground.

Much of the confusion in the center is expressed in the state of the white political parties. The United party has dissolved itself and re-appeared, in alliance with a smaller grouping, as the New Republican party. With about 25 seats it is still the official opposition but a shadow of its former self. Some of its supporters are turning toward the Progressive-Reform party with its philosophy of an integrated society moving steadily toward majority rule under a qualified franchise. Others, probably a majority, are frightened by this concept and are seeking refuge with the nationalists on the right. The Progressive-Reform party is trying hard to capture the middle ground. It has the backing of the Anglo-American industrial empire and other segments of the business community; the Anglican and Catholic churches are fellow travelers. It has a number of talented and dedicated people in its ranks and is making a strong bid for moderate black support, particularly that of Chief Gatsha Buthelezi and some of the more prominent urban blacks. With the demise of the United party, the Progressive-Reform party could emerge as the principal opposition to the Nationalists in the next election. Ironically, the people who are closest to the Progressive-Reform party in this polarizing process are those among the Afrikaner *verligtes* who share its belief that a qualitative change in the country's racial policies is essential if further bloodshed is to be avoided.

White moderates are showing schizoid tendencies under the strain. The press has been in the vanguard, calling passionately, sometimes hysterically, for change. The English-language newspapers go further than the Afrikaans in demanding an end to apartheid and a true dialogue between representatives of all races in a "National convention" on the lines of the convention that brought the Afrikaners and English together in 1909 and produced the constitution for the independent Union of South Africa. One major dissonant voice in the English chorus is the new Afrikaner-owned English-language daily, the *Citizen*, which broadly supports the government. It is a sign of the confused times that several of the Afrikaans newspapers are now to the Left of the *Citizen* and, while not as radical in their prescriptions as the majority of the English press, are calling for political rights for urban blacks and new multi-ethnic consultative mechanisms in the central government. This development, shocking to many Nationalists who have grown up with an Afrikaans press unswervingly loyal to the party, has worried the government.

The churches, long criticized for not taking a stronger lead against government policies, have cranked themselves into a posture of defiance. The Roman Catholics are integrating their schools at a cautious rate, and the Anglicans are planning to follow suit. The percentage of the total school population is minute—the Catholics educate only a little over 1 percent of all South African children in their private and fee-paying schools— but the policy runs directly counter to government doctrine. Pressure for change in the policy that governs multiracial (or "multi-ethnic") sports has received a favorable response at government level but has met resistance lower down in the clubs. The removal of "petty" discrimination—public signs, restrictions on the use of public facilities, and so on—has had a similarly checkered path. In an interview, Helen Suzman of the Progressive-Reform party accurately summed up what those petty apartheid reforms meant: "To the outside world—nothing at all; to the blacks in South Africa—very little; to the whites—a hell of a lot." There are genuine attempts by government, private groups, and individuals to improve not only the image of their society's race relations but also its substance. After a ten-year absence from South Africa, I found that Africans were treated much more politely by whites; they were better off, too, although the economic gap between the races appeared wider than ever. The government has begun to educate its sprawling bureaucracy to treat the black man with greater respect; the post office, for example, has sent out circulars to its white employees to that effect. Blacks, who used to be regarded as barely human— newspaper reports used to read: three people and ten natives were killed in the train disaster, etc.—now have their names prefixed by "Mr." in the press. Times are changing in South Africa, and it would be wrong to ignore the fact. But, as many visitors point out, racial tensions are more acute in the Republic than in Rhodesia, a country actually at war with black nationalism. The Soweto upheavals brought a rush on the gunshops and the formation of white vigilante groups as a new fear spread throughout the land. Emigration is increasing, new regulations have been introduced to plug the loopholes through which people have been getting their money out, and the property market has slumped.

The crisis has also stirred the business community, which is still dominated by English-speaking South Africans. Representative groups such as the Transvaal Chamber of Industries and the Association of Chambers of Commerce have sent critical memorandums to the government. The major industrialists have reacted by setting up an organization called the Urban Foundation, dedicated to improving the "quality of life" of the urban African, and is busying itself with projects such as financing home ownership in Soweto and the long-overdue electrification of the township. The business community—Afrikaners as well as English—has been particularly alarmed at the effect of the unrest on an already weakened economy and in the boardrooms of South Africa's major investors and trading partners. Business pressure on the government is not political nor does it represent a serious challenge, since it is largely the Afrikaner foot soldiers of industry, not its English captains, who sustain the National party's hold on power. But the pessimistic mood introduces another fluid element into the middle ground, and because of the crucial importance of the economy to the government's capacity to defend its policies, Vorster cannot afford to overlook it entirely.

How is the government reacting to these developments? And what kind of pressure produces what kind of change in South Africa? Afrikaners often talk of their willingness to fight a lone battle if necessary, and their history lends credibility to the threat. But they need auxiliaries and this implies a shifting pattern of deals and alliances, not overtly political, more usually based on mutual economic interest. The government's usual reaction to pressure is to confront it forcefully, then temporize (this is the stage at which commissions are appointed), and finally, if there is no alternative,

search for a compromise in which there will be some elements of concession.

There seem to be two nerve centers which, when touched, activate this cycle of response. The first is a major threat to the economy. The Durban strikes in 1973, widespread, prolonged, and potentially harmful to the whole economy, were a good example.* The government handled the strikes with great caution, refraining from its usual heavy-handed tactics and eventually granting the wage-increase that the black workers had demanded. Again, whenever there is a serious shortage of white skilled labor, the government allows blacks to move into jobs hitherto barred to them, a move that bends both statutory and customary law but permits the wheels of industry to turn smoothly.

The second nerve center is foreign sensitivity. The image South Africa presents to the West is an important concern of the government in Pretoria, and a large amount of money and energy is spent promoting it. But international pressure is rarely a force for innovative change within South Africa; rather it is a factor for curbing reactive excess. Pretoria, however, is much more responsive to external pressures when the target lies outside its frontiers as its flexibility over Rhodesia with Kissinger and over South-West Africa with the five Western nations' "contact" group has shown. Annoyed by the South African press's criticism of the way it handled the black unrest, the government introduced legislation early in 1977 that would have effectively censored it. The unprecedented criticism of government policies in the normally loyal Afrikaans newspapers made matters worse. An outcry arose in South Africa, but the decisive factor in persuading the government to suspend the measure for a year (during which time the press will have to behave "responsibly") was almost certainly the damage such a move would have inflicted on South Africa's image abroad, destroying its justifiable claim to have the freest press in Africa.

There is no shortage of other examples. The clash with the churches over school desegregation has been headed off by talks and compromise at the provincial level, while party ideologues have continued to fulminate about apartheid orthodoxies on the national stage. The churches' international connections would make a direct confrontation embarrassing for the government and counterproductive in view of its much-publicized desire to rid the country of "racial discrimination."** The Soweto riots produced a vivid example of the government making concessions mainly because it was worried about the country's reputation abroad. Before the upheaval began, the government had been unbending over the use of Afrikaans as a medium of instruction in African schools, despite much local pressure to

---

* Within the three-month period from January to March, 1973, there were 160 wildcat strikes in Natal involving 146 industries and over 60,000 black workers.

** There is a special irony here: when black American and Malawian diplomats were first allowed to work in South Africa, Pretoria asked the Catholics to admit the diplomats' children to their then all-white schools. The Catholics agreed and now find themselves in the position of the supplicant.

end the practice. The students with their placards, their courage, and, in the end, their dead projected the grievance onto an international screen, making the government appear rigid and more than a little ridiculous. Vorster backed down, again with ominous *verkrampte* noises on his Right. Two other grievances—home ownership and the electrification of Soweto—on which the government had been equally unresponsive before the riots were met in full after them. Furthermore, the marked change in police tactics in dealing with student demonstrations in Soweto—plastic shields and restraint have replaced rifles and trigger-happiness—has had much to do with the reaction of foreign governments and overseas public opinion to the police's murderous handling of the earlier upheavals.

Sports, an area in which considerable change has taken place as the result of direct international pressure, is in a category of its own. White South Africans, particularly the Afrikaners, are obsessed with sports; international rugby matches are followed with the gravity and anguish normally associated with a foreign war. Harried by international boycotts and under considerable pressure at home, the government has made a number of major concessions to the ideal of mixed sports, without having completely achieved that goal, but has had to fight a rear-guard action with conservatives in both the Afrikaner and English communities.

Of course, the two pressure points that seem to produce positive results—the interests of the economy and the country's overseas image—are linked. The economy is critically dependent upon foreign capital for growth, and the supply of foreign capital is, in view of South Africa's pariah status, highly sensitive to the nuances of the government's behavior in every purlieu of its authority. Also, any kind of political upheaval strikes in both directions, simultaneously damaging local production and undermining foreign confidence. Mobil's chairman in South Africa estimated that the Soweto riots reduced the country's gross national product by between 1 and 1.5 percent in 1976.

But there are clearly defined limits to the government's flexibility. It will brook no direct challenge to its authority. Concessions have been made to the students, but the leadership has been ruthlessly dispersed and suppressed. Second, social and economic change within the framework of separate development is permissible; political alterations to the structure are not. Admission of a small number of black middle-class children to a small number of white middle-class schools can be tolerated, while granting political rights to urban Africans remains anathema. Buthelezi, the avowed enemy of apartheid, can continue to attack the government from the platform the system has given him, but Matanzima, Vorster's friend and collaborator, is ignored when he asserts that Xhosas who were born, and want to stay, in South Africa should not be compelled to become Transkei citizens. Black workers can take over "white" jobs when there are not enough whites available (technically an illegal procedure) but cannot have registered unions (technically legal) because that would upset the white workers and strengthen the organizational muscle of black power in the heart of the economy where the government fears it most. "A meaningful role for

blacks in their *local* affairs in the metropolitan areas" (my italics) was promised by Vorster in a letter to the Association of Chambers of Commerce
and can be conceded, but those same blacks are being deprived of their
South African citizenship as the Bantustans become independent.

The pattern for the future, at least for the arbitrary period of five years
that most thinking South Africans have allotted for peaceful change, is apparent in today's policies. The government is making its own belated bid
for good will in the center. A new constitutional deal for Coloureds and Indians, giving them their own parliaments and a closer consultative link with
the white leadership, has been introduced. The black townships are going
to receive wider self-governing powers; home ownership, after many false
starts, is beginning to go ahead; more money is to be spent on black education so that it can eventually be made compulsory and free, a status that
white education acquired many years ago; greater autonomy—and more
money—is to be given to the Bantustans, whether they opt for independence or not; legislation extending the benefits of workers' compensation
to all races—blacks were previously excluded—has been introduced in Parliament; Soweto, at last, is to receive electricity (only 25 percent of the
township currently has it), although much of the credit should go to the
private sector, which has prepared the plans and is raising the financing;
Coloureds and Indians will be allowed access to industrial zones outside
their own group areas; and the government has declared it an objective of
policy to eliminate "wage and salary differentials based purely on race."

The darker thread in the design is the relentless pursuit of "grand
apartheid." Internal and external pressures may well produce more social
and economic concessions like those listed above, but such pressures are
unlikely (at the level of their present intensity, whether they take the form
of more urban unrest or a further cooling of foreign investors) to trigger
significant political changes in the system. In this holy area, the sacristy of
government policy, Vorster is not prepared to move an inch to please
those caught in the middle of the South African conundrum. The facts
speak for themselves. Bophuthatswana is to follow the Transkei into independence; the pass laws, the lasso of apartheid, are being tightened by
heavier penalties and greater vigilance; removals of Africans, Coloureds,
and Indians from white areas are continuing; tougher measures for clearing
out illegal squatters have been enacted and are being enforced. Bannings,
imprisonment without trial, torture, and murder (unexplained deaths and
"suicides" in well-guarded prisons)—the "big three" in the category of sins
against human rights—have mutilated the leadership of the black consciousness and labor movements. Improvements in the conditions and pay
of the black labor force may come; but a fully recognized and freely functioning black trade-union movement is a political nonstarter, and equal pay
for equal work, given the artificially inflated rate of white wages and the
depressed economy, is an economic impossibility in the foreseeable future.

If further evidence is needed of the South African government's determination to pursue the main themes of separate development come hell
or high water, it can be found very simply in the nature of its priorities. A

nation's concerns, like an individual's or a family's, are usually accurately reflected in the way it allocates and spends its money. Defense, at $1.9 billion, is by far the biggest item in the 1977-78 budget, rising by 21 percent over the previous year and consuming 18 percent of the total for the current year. Spending on black education has risen substantially, but at $135 million in the same budget, it lags a long way behind the $350 million designated for white education. The government has earmarked $117 million for a separate black television service, which is scheduled to be ready in 1980. Yet, the *Washington Post* reported that, according to an official on the board that administers Soweto, the $50 million required to build 20,000 houses urgently needed to alleviate the overcrowding problem is not available. "We don't have a cent," the official said. "We are completely broke." More money ($138 million) is going as aid to the independent Transkei than is to be spent on black education ($135 million) in South Africa itself during the fiscal year 1977-78.

Even within the parameters of social and economic reform, that area on which the government will increasingly concentrate as pressures intensify and in which many Afrikaner reformists believe apartheid can be invested with a moral respectability, there are precise limits defined by the peculiar nature of South African society. These demarcation lines run around the central concerns of Africans' daily lives. The most important are land ownership, housing, freedom of movement, jobs, and schooling. Under apartheid, whether it is Vorster's or his successor's brand, it is hard to see change coming fast enough to satisfy the blacks' rising aspirations and check the dangerous polarization that has already begun. It is possible that adjustments in the Bantustans' boundaries will provide them with more land, but the proportion of the total land and resources is unlikely to be materially altered. Long leases for township houses are now available to Africans, but the land on which the houses are built will remain the property of the government. To administer apartheid, the government has to maintain the pass system, the single most-hated feature of the whole scheme among Africans. The security apparatus also needs such a monitoring mechanism. Suggestions that the pass laws should be administered more humanely, treating infringements as civil misdemeanors instead of criminal offenses, have been rejected by the government. Labor reforms depend heavily on the state of the economy. In times of expansion, wages and job opportunities improve, as the experience of the early seventies showed. But recession means a tighter labor market and tougher action by the government and white trade unions to enforce job reservation. Government concessions in response to repeated calls by different sectors of commerce and industry to recognize black trade unions have fallen short of that goal, and are likely to continue to do so.* Although higher on its list of priorities, the

---

* The government has drafted legislation designed to give black workers from the same industry, and the same area, representation on an elected committee for that section of the labor force. However, each committee will have to be approved by the minister of labor, and its members will have to be full-time workers, thus ruling out the possibility of professional union officials.

education of Africans is still the poor relation in the budget, with ten times
more being spent on the education of every white than on every black child. "Petty apartheid" will undoubtedly continue to be eroded, but real apartheid, notably the segregation of schools, residential areas, and commercial zones—the very essence of the system—will remain inviolate.

In the broader perspective, Vorster is both a prisoner of his separate-development policies and a victim of a straitened economy. This situation has its more lunatic aspects, such as the government lavishing over one-hundred million dollars on a separate black television facility, which the Africans did not ask for and do not want, while the white building and engineering unions are taking measures to bar blacks from jobs, which they do want. But it also raises the question of government priorities in the future. The Johannesburg *Financial Mail* (January 28,1977) stated the dilemma.

> An economy averaging only 2% to 3% annual growth (the current figure) will not be able to meet simultaneously the demands of escalating defence spending, vast new investment in transport, steel, oil-from-coal, power generation, uranium enrichment and so on. And this does not even include the much higher spending needed to improve both the quality of life of urban blacks and the viability of the homelands. Which will be sacrificed?

With pressures mounting, it is not hard to imagine where the government's axe will fall.

There is another problem, that of growth itself. If the economy picks up, foreign capital resumes its flow, and growth reaches the government's target of 5.75 percent a year, by 1980 there will be a need for some 3.8 million more skilled workers, of which the white labor force will be able to supply only about half, leaving a shortfall of almost 2 million. The choice will be between curtailing the rate of growth or turning over to Africans jobs traditionally reserved for whites, thus binding the blacks more inextricably than ever to the economy. The other, and more likely, possibility is that the economy will fail to grow at the required rate (real economic growth for 1976 was only 1.4 percent, the lowest since World War II) and the government will be faced with the problem of trying to absorb the 175,000 to 200,000 Africans who enter the job market every year.

The government sincerely wants to mesh the loyalties of all sections of the population to face the external threat it sees mounting outside its frontiers. It would like to recruit blacks into combat units of its army, as the Rhodesians have done; it would like to engage the black South Africans' deep love of country (a patriotism shared by all races but by no means unquestioningly at the government's disposal); it wishes, no doubt, that black rugby fans would cheer the home team instead of the visitors; and it keenly wants to be seen by all as the guardian of ethnic diversity rather than the upholder of white privilege. But it is not prepared to pay the price. Some observers think the time for reconciliation and compromise is already past. Laurence Gander, a distinguished former editor of the *Rand Daily Mail*, wrote, at the height of the township upheavals in the September 8, 1976, issue of the *Rand Daily Mail:*

> It is a struggle of classic simplicity—between those who hold power, which means the Afrikaners, and those who aspire to power, which means the Africans. The rest of us who neither possess power nor can aspire to it are mere bystanders, wringing our hands in helpless rage or anguish, shouting disregarded accusations and advice at the contenders.

He is probably right in the long run. In Rhodesia and South-West Africa, the struggle has already reached the stage of "classic simplicity"; its end is predictable and inevitable. In the Republic, the adage that the situation in South Africa is catastrophic but not yet serious, implying that the crisis is containable in the short term but disastrous in the long, retains its kernel of truth. There is still room for maneuver, but failing significant progress in the immediate future, the middle ground will no longer be a haven for compromise but a desolate no-man's-land. Once the battle lines between Afrikaner and African have been drawn, there will be no turning back, although, given the inherent strength and tenacity of Afrikaner nationalism, the outcome may be different: partition rather than black rule.

There is always a danger in underestimating the staying power of white minority governments in Africa. Sir Harold Wilson, the former British prime minister, predicted in 1966 that the world would witness the capitulation of Ian Smith's breakaway government in "a matter of weeks not months." Smith, it transpired, was only at the beginning of a long run of successful defiance. It took fourteen years of inconclusive but sapping guerrilla warfare in Angola and a decade of the same in Mozambique to produce a change of government in Lisbon. The Republic of South Africa is, in every sense, a tougher nut to crack. And the task of assessing the balance of forces in the struggle for power there is made doubly difficult by the fact that it has been shielded for so long by the white buffer zone and by its own physical strength. In the past, the South African protagonists have tended to look beyond the country and the region for the means with which to wage their struggle and for their ultimate salvation. Thus the whites turned to the West for arms, money, technology, immigrants, and, in the event of disaster, physical support. Similarly, the blacks sought a denial of these things by the West and moral and material backing from the African states, the United Nations, and the communist bloc. Now the situation has changed. The decisive factors that determine the critical strengths and vulnerabilities of the adversaries in the South African drama are no longer international but national and regional. International pressures, or the lack of them, will still play a role in the theater of conflict but they will be ancillary to the internal dynamics of the situation. It is true that Soviet, and probably Cuban, military power will be involved, but both their size and the use to which they are put will be determined by the actors themselves and the important supporting cast in the black belt of independent states ringing the Republic.

It also seems likely that the balance of international pressures, whether buttresses of the South African fortress or siege weapons against it, will not change substantially in the immediate future. Pretoria will continue to be able to buy most of the arms it needs and to make the rest; Iran and other countries will continue to supply it with oil; the International Monetary Fund will not demonetize gold and thus drastically weaken the Republic's main source of foreign exchange; the West will not support mandatory economic sanctions; and, assuming the Soviet-Cuban threat remains one of proxy and does not transform itself into a direct confrontation, the West will not become militarily involved on either side. In short, the siege that Pretoria is expecting will intensify, but the ring of attackers will not be complete nor will the supply lines of the defenders be cut. It looks rather as if history may repeat itself, with the Afrikaner pitted against the African in the old struggle for the land. Auxiliaries will be involved, local in the case of the Afrikaner and regional in the case of the African, but that is how it was in the past, too. The difference this time will be that the black man will also have a gun.

Is there then any role for the West? The chances of producing an evolutionary and bloodless solution to the South African problem seem to me to be slim. If the West were prepared to use the leverage theoretically at its disposal there might be some hope. But because of a number of constraints, principally connected with the free interplay of special interest groups in democratic societies, those levers remain theoretical. The West therefore has to confront the situation with one hand tied behind its back. Its attitude, given the mood of the times, will probably be guided by a mixture of realism, self-interest and morality. Realism will dictate a closer but not slavish adherence to Africa's desires in the matter; self-interest will curb extreme pressures against South Africa; and morality will ensure that the Republic becomes even more isolated.

These contradictions and the limitations they impose do not completely preclude a Western policy. There is one small loophole still available through which Western influence may be directed with, admittedly, an equally small chance of success, but it is worth a try all the same. This entails giving succor to the South African middle ground where a large number of whites, browns, and blacks are bucking up and down on their rollercoaster of hope and foreboding. The Progressive-Reform party, big business, Buthelezi, the Coloured and Indian leaders, prominent urban Africans, a huge segment of the working black population, and even some Afrikaners are there waiting.

The time-scale is short. Revolution is not yet round the corner in South Africa but a revolutionary situation is developing. The next five years or so—a little longer than the life of the first Carter administration—will be crucial. South Africans who oppose the government's policies are asking for pressure from the West, not for solutions. It is clear, in terms of general principles, what the majority of South Africans want: full political participation, equality before the law, abolition of racially discriminatory legislation, the ending of inequitable labor practices and so on. But it would be arrogant for anyone foreign to that ferociously complex country to prescribe the constitutional remedy; that, surely, is the prerogative of the South Africans themselves. And whatever they choose—majority rule, federalism, confederalism, even partition or apartheid—is their right and it should be respected by the world community.

There seemed to be some initial confusion about the aim of United States policy in South Africa, but after his discussions with Vorster in Vienna in May, 1977, Vice-President Walter Mondale made it clear at a press conference that the "full political participation" which he had been talking about was the same thing as one man, one vote. "Every citizen," he said, "should have the right to vote and every vote should be equally weighed." Majority rule may be the best solution or it may not, but no one in the Republic has yet had a chance to discuss it or vote on it. Unlike the situation in the American South where the businessmen were the oppressors who held power, business in South Africa is largely in the hands of the people who have no real power and want change anyway (the English), while power is in the exclusive control of those who are less vulnerable to such economic pressures (the Afrikaners).

Andrew Young, the U.S. ambassador to the United Nations, has urged that additional pressure should be exercised by the multinational corporations operating in the Republic. But these companies are also subject to counter-pressures from the South African government under the country's tough commercial and security laws. For the sake of harmony and continued investment, Pretoria will probably not block some reforms such as the code of standards which a number of American companies have adopted, pledging themselves to improve the conditions of their black workers. However, the government is unlikely to bow to demands which cut across fundamental policy—recognition of black unions, for example—or permit locally-based multinationals a special license when it comes to matters which it considers impinge on national security. A good example of the restraints imposed on the multinationals came when Mobil's head office in New York announced that it could not obtain information about its South African-based subsidiary's alleged breach of United Nations sanctions by supplying oil to Rhodesia because the Republic's Official Secrets Act prevented it.

There seems to be only one acceptable theme for outside pressure and that is the launching of a meaningful dialogue between all the races in South Africa. Many people in the country, from widely different political perspectives, have been calling for a national convention for many years. Such a move would engage the support of the front-line African states, for it would be in their own national interest to seek a peaceful and negotiated solution in South Africa, as it has been in their interest to do so in Rhodesia and South-West Africa, because functioning, stable neighbors reinforce their own fragile cohesion and stability, while chaos or prolonged armed struggle weaken them. Revolutionary means may be necessary to achieve a South African dialogue, but there is no indication that the African presidents demand a revolutionary outcome. (Even Marxist Mozambique threw its weight behind multilateral talks on the Rhodesian problem.) Focusing on the center zone also has the advantage of denying some leverage to the Soviet Union, which, although committed to both revolutionary means and revolutionary ends and ready to fill a vacuum should one be created—as it was in Angola—cannot afford to ignore the priorities of African front-line strategy.

Even Vorster would find himself hard pressed to escape the logic of an interracial dialogue, because that is precisely what he persuaded Ian Smith to do in Rhodesia by releasing the jailed black nationalists so that they could discuss a common future. He often repeats that it is up to all the peoples of South-West Africa to decide the future of their country. Does he not believe that in the end Nelson Mandela on Robben Island and Robert Sobukwe in Kimberley—as well as Chief Buthelezi in KwaZulu and perhaps even Chief Matanzima in the Transkei—should also take part in deciding the destiny of their country?

Given the limitations of Western leverage, the most likely pressures brought to bear would be diplomatic and financial. The South African government is vulnerable, and measures such as restriction of credit and loans and the withholding of new investment would have some impact on its economic strength. They would also probe a possible but as yet untested weakness in the defenses of Afrikanerdom. This is the effect of a reduced standard of living on a people now 90 percent urbanized and whose younger generation has by and large never known poverty and hardship, a phenomenon one observer has called the "soft underbelly of Afrikaner nationalism." Among American policy-makers, Andrew Young, in particular, believes this area to be crucial in the process of change, and it will be interesting to see if the Afrikaners' pocket is as sensitive as their Southern counterparts' was in the United States. Coupled with these measures would be the need to convince the whites that there would be no Western support if, as a result of Pretoria's policies, civil war came. The whites of southern Africa are tenacious in their belief that despite Angola, despite Rhodesia, and despite South-West Africa, the U.S. Cavalry will come galloping out of the sunset to save them when all appears to be lost.

The reaction in Pretoria to such Western pressures would be principally psychological, producing dismay and anger. South Africa desires, above all, a recognition by the United States of a community of interest between the two countries which would lessen the Republic's isolation and secure a measure of cooperation, albeit low-keyed, in defense and intelligence matters. South Africa also wants the United States to pay more attention to the value of its strategic geography and minerals and accept Pretoria's assessment that together they constitute a prime target of Soviet aggrandisement.

The greatest shock delivered by the Carter administration, apart from Mondale's statement that the U.S. government has officially endorsed majority rule as its solution to South Africa's problems, is that Washington is showing signs of seeing the strategic issue completely the other way around: that South Africa, because of its racial policies, is a liability instead of an asset in the struggle against the growth of communist influence in southern Africa.

In tactical terms, South Africans regard the application of mandatory UN economic sanctions as the worst tangible threat that the international community can hold over their heads in the near future. Such sanctions, in spite of the likelihood that they would not be effective, would be regarded as a disaster in Pretoria because they would drive the Republic further into isolation and give an aura of legitimacy to subsequent hostile actions. A mandatory arms embargo, the more likely first step in view of Western domestic restraints and commercial caution, is feared less because the country is already subjected to a number of arms bans and is self-sufficient for much of its needs.

But it would be unrealistic to expect a sudden change of heart by the South African government. Indeed, it might well react by pushing ahead even faster with its apartheid policies and becoming more uncompromising in its rhetoric. The facts show that the government is already unbending on the central aspects of apartheid and it is already pursuing its goals with the greatest speed it can muster. Nevertheless, Western pressures linked to a call for a national convention without a constitutional prescription would put the government in something of a quandary. It would also give hope to those struggling to hold the middle ground. Finally, it would be welcomed by the African states, which do not expect miracles from the West but do want a clear statement of principle on South Africa, backed by visible pressures. And any political bonus for the West in Africa is an automatic political deduction for the Soviet Union.

The experience of African countries that had large white settler communities, such as Algeria, Kenya, Mozambique, Angola, Rhodesia, and South-West Africa, has demonstrated that powerful ruling minorities do not move in the direction of sharing either economic privilege or political control unless physical pressure is exerted on them. Even those controlled by metropolitan powers needed this stimulus to convince them of the need to face the realities of African nationalism. Assuming that sufficient physical pressure will not be applied to South Africa by the West, and assuming that the Nationalist government will not move in a meaningful way to meet black aspirations, then the rapid growth of black revolutionary forces seems inevitable. Military victory by these forces is neither likely nor necessary. The

FLN did not beat the French nor did the Mau Mau defeat the British; the
Zimbabwe guerrillas are equally unlikely to overthrow the Rhodesian government, and SWAPO can no more defeat the South African army than El Fatah can beat the Israelis. But African nationalists know they can lose every battle and still win the war. It will be surprising if the Afrikaners do not eventually grasp that point, for it is the lesson of their own history. They lost on the battlefield to the British but they finally won that war. In the end, numbers count.

But, people will say, South Africa is different. Well, it is and it isn't. It is different because Afrikaner nationalism, a strange and unique creation, has entrenched itself deeply at the toe-end of Africa and cannot transplant itself somewhere else. It is different because there is no metropolitan force involved, because the country has a sophisticated economy, a treasure chest of important minerals, a much larger white population than any of Africa's other settler countries, and a uniquely strategic position between the Indian and Atlantic oceans. It is also different because it has begun to dissect the country, on a small scale, in an attempt to syphon off black pressure.

But it is not different in essence from the other colonial struggles in Africa; in truth, it is all of them writ large. The Afrikaners were originally settlers from another world; part of the land they occupied was only sparsely inhabited but much of it was contested bitterly by the Africans who were already there.* To Africa, the Republic is, in the words of the Lusaka Manifesto, an "independent, sovereign state and member of the United Nations," but its government has forfeited its legitimacy by its racist policies. South Africa's blacks do not accept the distinctions that others make between their country's status and other nations in Africa. Most of them believe the Afrikaners and the English took their land and that they have more right to it than the whites, especially the hundreds of thousands of new immigrants. They believe that their South African nationalism—not the tribal version of it catered to under separate development—is as valid as the Afrikaners' and they stress that it has been functioning on an organized basis since 1912, two years after the country became independent. The fact that there are many more whites in South Africa than elsewhere on the continent does not, in the Africans' view, alter the fact that they are a privileged minority with an exclusive hold on political and economic power. The country's economic infrastructure, resources, and strategic geography merely highlight the powerlessness and deprivation that the unrepresented majority suffer. The whites' argument that the blacks are infinitely better off than most of their brothers in Africa cuts no ice, for the same reason that it does no good to tell a poor American of Mexican or Puerto Rican origin that his cousins back home are poorer than he is. Black South Africans, naturally enough, compare their conditions with those of white South Africans, beside whom they live and work, not with Tanza-

---

* The best documented account of who was where in the early days of white settlement is in the *Oxford History of South Africa*, Monica Wilson and Leonard Thompson, eds., 2 vols. (New York: Oxford University Press, 1969 and 1971).

nians or Zaireans, whom they have never seen. The Bantustan policy is no answer for those who feel themselves part of the whole country, for those who live and work in the factories and farms and want to share the material things that their labor has produced, for those who have neither family connection nor work nor land in the homelands, for those who were never asked but bluntly told that this was the final solution. For these black South Africans there is no qualitative difference in their status from the black Kenyans or Angolans under their colonial masters. There is, however, a difference of degree: their condition is worse because their oppressor is more determined and more fearful.

But how determined and how fearful? Are the Afrikaners bluffing or are they deadly serious? At the moment, Afrikanerdom, though apprehensive, still feels strong and secure. The *volk* as a whole has yet to be persuaded that it is in its own best interests to introduce sweeping changes in order to meet black demands. When the day of enlightenment comes, the changes may also come, though whether or not they will be too late is another matter. With Vorster and his generation, it is hard to imagine new initiatives or directions, trapped as they are within the constraints of their own narrow concept of *kragdadiheid* (literally, "strength" or "power"; metaphorically, "iron-fistedness") and within the even narrower limitations of their thirty-year-old policy of separate development. They are men entering their final years, moving at an ox-wagon pace in a jet age. Every political instinct they possess tells them to hold and to fight. John Vorster, they say, plays chess for relaxation, but now the game on the South African board is in deadly earnest, although both the chess and the *laager* metaphor should perhaps be superseded by the image of the Afrikaners' Dutch ancestors methodically building their dikes to hold back the stormy sea. The Afrikaners have historically feared a sea, too; but for them it has been the human tide of black nationalism. They are building their dikes with an almost biblical determination and it is possible to detect the cadences of the Old Testament in their rhetoric. Vorster, in his New Year's eve speech (1977), reminded his people that "we still have a long way to go to fulfill our calling and God in his mercy will not cripple us before we have walked the road which he has ordained us to do." This matches well with the all-or-nothing syndrome that many South African whites, and not only Afrikaners, have slipped into. It is the government's road or majority rule, they say; there is nothing in between. And majority rule to an Afrikaner, whether *verkramp* or *verlig,* is like the Palestinians' vision of a secular Palestine to an Israeli. This brings one to the Afrikaner's bottom line, and it has been stated succinctly in the *Manchester Guardian Weekly* (April 3, 1977) by Connie Mulder, Vorster's most likely successor: "Many things are negotiable [within the apartheid system], but two things we will fight and die for: the identity of our nation and our right to be in Africa. Political decisions affecting these will remain in our hands exclusively in order to ensure that someone else cannot decide that we [the Afrikaners] are swept away." In short, the Afrikaner only recognizes two alternatives: white salvation through separate development and white perdition through its abandonment. The Africans are equally determined. In an editorial the November 25, 1976, issue of the *World*, South Africa's only black daily newspaper, said: "Mr. Vorster has given an undertaking that this country will not change its policy. We want to give an undertaking that our people are determined that the policy will be changed because they do not accept it and will not be a party to their own humiliation."

In view of the limitations of Western power and the bleak perception of the Afrikaner's alternatives, what is likely to happen in the short term, say three-to-five years? While the National party remains a captive of the economic interests and social prejudices of its rank and file, as seems highly probable, there will be little chance of the *verligte* reformists seizing the heights of power or of materially influencing the direction of government policies. Military coups, from the Right or from the Left, are similarly improbable. The most likely development will be a more authoritarian government under the present leadership, whether or not Vorster remains in office. An executive presidential system of government is a strong possibility, but the preoccupations of Afrikanerdom's leaders will continue to be the cohesion of the tribe's institutions, the solidarity of the party, and the consolidation of power in the hands of those chosen to lead. The short term, therefore, is likely to witness an era of growing authoritarianism in Afrikaner government, politics, and society. In the middle ground, Buthelezi is busily mustering his forces and may launch a civil disobedience campaign among his black followers while maintaining contact with the liberal whites. Buthelezi is a man who believes in the necessity for building political structures and Vorster is a man who is experienced in destroying them. There could be a head-on clash. The Zulu chief is also a target for the black nationalists, and his position, personal as well as political, is likely to become increasingly vulnerable. A general strike by black workers remains the Africans' most potent weapon, but it is not likely to be used unless the economic situation becomes so desperate that the black labor force will decide that it has nothing to lose. Wildcat strikes, stoppages, boycotts, and stay-aways will probably occur, as they have always done, but at a rising tempo. More young blacks are likely to leave the country to join the guerrilla forces, and the black consciousness movement will make more converts.

What if the center fails to hold and South Africa, after that grace period, slides into racial conflict? Authoritarianism could easily turn into straight dictatorship. White South Africans—including the Afrikaners—cherish their British legacy of parliamentary institutions. But part of the Afrikaners' pragmatism consists of being able to devise radical solutions to meet radical situations, and there is already much talk of "consensus politics" and of the inadequacy of the "Westminster system." The generals, whether they like it or not, will inevitably move into the limelight, although the tradition of a nonpolitical army will act as a restraint. By this stage, the middle-ground will be as ineffective in South Africa as it is in Rhodesia today. The "classic struggle"—Afrikaner versus African—will be engaged.

And if, in the long term, the situation deteriorates further and civil war engulfs South Africa? Partition in closely interwoven societies (Cyprus,

Lebanon, Ireland) is never thought possible until it happens, for the simple reason that it is invariably the result of civil war. No one wants it ideally, no one really accepts it, but it finally occurs because neither side can defeat the other and the alternative is endless bloodshed. If Connie Mulder and the majority of the Afrikaners for whom he speaks mean what they say when they talk of fighting and dying for the identity of their nation and their right to be in Africa, and assuming black power eventually becomes strong enough to present a physical challenge to the Afrikaners, then a partitioned South Africa seems a highly probable outcome. The Afrikaners now working on partition plans are not so unrealistic as many people think. The logical conclusion of separate development is partition anyway, but the partitionists rightly argue that 13 percent of the land and virtually none of the country's infrastructure or resources are already totally inadequate for the 18 million blacks. How much more inadequate will these be when, within a single generation, the African population will have doubled? Partition will, of course, mean disruption, sacrifice, a harder life for the Afrikaner tribe in a much smaller state. But that is the price they will have to pay for their ethnic exclusiveness, for their continued existence in Africa. There is an element of flexibility within the Afrikaner psyche that may tolerate such reduced circumstances, although they will have to accept that partition, whether it comes peacefully or bloodily, may still not be the end of the affair. The Afrikaners can no longer trek; there is nowhere to trek to except the dusty road back to the Cape. They have to dominate, deal, or die. So far they have chosen the path of domination, ignoring or absorbing internal and external pressures. There is no sign of their turning off that path; but when they do, they may jettison dogma and work for compromise, as their forebears did in similar circumstances, displaying once again the pragmatism that has allowed them to survive for so long in an alien environment.

The Afrikaners are still haunted by two historical images, their own ox-wagon *laagers* which protected them from the Africans, and the British concentration camps which killed so many of their women and children. But in following the apartheid road "ordained by God" rigidly and blindly, the images have become confused to the point where the *laager* has become a prison of the mind. To them the road is straight and clear. To others in the beloved country it is the way of false prophets, leading nowhere but to conflict and bloodshed. The South African house is not built on sand, but it is mortally divided within.

Footnotes

CHAPTER I

1. T. Dunbar Moody used the phrase in his book *The Rise of Afrikanerdom* (Berkeley and Los Angeles: University of California Press, 1975).

2. This survey was carried out by Anglo-American, a giant conglomerate, which conducts a similar exercise every five years. The results were given to me on a confidential basis.

3. Quoted in *To the Point* (Johannesburg), 10 December 1976.

4. *Christian Science Monitor*, 2 February 1977.

5. *Washington Post*, 11 January 1977.

6. Erika Theron Commission (1976), Recommendation no. 178, pp. 512-13.

7. André du Toit, who teaches political science at Stellenbosch University, presented an interesting paper to a meeting organized by the Progressive-Reform party in November, 1976. These comments and those by Professor Barry Dean are from this paper, which is in the author's possession.

8. This interesting survey was printed in full in *Optima* 24 (1974), Number 2, pp. 57-65.

9. These remarks appeared in the South African press and were reported in the "Update" section of *Africa Report*, September/October 1976.

CHAPTER II

1. For an excellent and comprehensive article on the Coloureds, see Leon Weaver, *Africa Report*, September/October 1976.

2. Fatima Meer, "An Indian's View of Apartheid" in N.J. Rhoodie, ed., *South African Dialogue* (Johannesburg: McGraw-Hill, 1972).

3. J. L. Sadie, *Projection of the South African Population, 1970-2020* (Johannesburg, 1973). The figures for the whites assume an annual net increase of 30,000 immigrants.

4. Francis Wilson, "Political Implications for Blacks of Economic Changes" in Leonard Thompson and Jeffrey Butler, eds., *Change in Contemporary South Africa* (Berkeley and Los Angeles: University of California Press, 1975).

5. Stanley Uys in the *Observer* (London), 2 January 1977.

1. See articles in the *Financial Mail* (Johannesburg), 5 November 1976, 11 November 1976, and 18 February 1977.

2. The South African minister of defense, P.W. Botha, later made a statement in Parliament listing his country's casualties in Angola "from 14th July 1975 to 23rd January 1976."

3. The best military account of the Angolan war so far is Robert Moss's four-part series in the London *Sunday Telegraph* (30 January, 6 February, 13 February, and 20 February 1977). Moss is less convincing on the nature of the American involvement and the diplomatic complexities of the crisis.

4. This reconstruction is based on interviews with military, government, and journalistic sources in South Africa, November and December 1976.

5. South African fliers fought in Korea, but no ground troops were involved.

6. Bill Anderson's testimony to the Council for Namibia in the United Nations, September 1976. Anderson, a South African conscript who later left the country, was in Grootfontein at the time of the Angolan intervention.

7. *Armed Forces*, vol. 1, no. 4 (April 1976), column authored by "Diogenes."

CHAPTER IV

1. Introduction to *White Paper on Defence* (Cape Town: Government Printer, 1973).

2. Edouard Bustin, "South Africa's Foreign Policy Alternatives and Deterrence Needs" in Onkar Marwah and Ann Schulz, eds., *Nuclear Proliferation and the Near-Nuclear Countries* (Cambridge, Massachusetts: Ballinger Publishing Co., 1975), p. 213.

3. These figures are from *The Military Balance, 1976-77* (London: International Institute for Strategic Studies, 1977).

4. Bustin, *op. cit.*, p. 221.

5. *Ibid.*, pp. 223-24.

6. South African government figures, given in "Climate for Enterprise" (Pretoria: Department of Information, 1976).

7. Extracts from this report were quoted in *Journal of Commerce*, 7 April 1977.

8. "Special Report: SA 2000," *Financial Mail* (Johannesburg), 8 April 1977.

9. *Ibid.*

10. *Financial Mail* (Johannesburg), 19 July 1974; and economic sources in South Africa.

11. *Journal of Commerce*, 30 August 1976. This loan was backed with collateral of 6.25 million ounces of gold at the rate of $80 an ounce: a total value of $500 million.

12. *Africa Bureau Fact Sheet: The Role of Iran in South Africa*, no. 44 (London, November-December 1975).